Best Wishes

Richard

The Giant-Killers

Wrexham AFC, 1974–99
a fan's view

Richard Partington

bridge
books

Wrexham

First published in Wales by
BRIDGE BOOKS
61 Park Avenue
Wrexham
LL12 7AW

A CIP catalogue entry for this book is available
from the British Library.

ISBN 1-872424-95-3

Printed and bound by
MFP
Manchester

For
Trace
Daniel, Steven,
Mum and Dad

Acknowledgements

To my wife Trace for her support, encouragement, patience, love and much more. And to our sons Daniel and Steven for their love.

To Mum and Dad and all my family. Special thanks to Dad for taking me one Saturday a long time ago to a place called The Racecourse; and for sharing the elation and despair and all that is in-between that is being a Wrexham fan.

To Alister Williams for a dream come true.

To North Wales Newspapers for allowing access to their collection of photographs published in the *Wrexham Leader* and the *Evening Leader*.

To Nick Hornby for kindly allowing me to quote from his brilliant book, *Fever Pitch* (Victor Gollancz Ltd.).

To the many correspondents who have covered Wrexham over the years from the Evening Leader, Wrexham Leader, Shropshire Star, Daily Post, Radio Wales and Marcher Sound, in particular Dave Lovett, Les Chamberlain, the late Ron Challoner, Ian Gwyn Hughes and Oliver Hydes who have kept me informed and involved.

To Peter Jones, Gareth M. Davies, Anthony Jones and other supporters who have done so much to research and promote the history of the club.

To all those players who have pulled on a red shirt over the last 28 years and filled my memory with so many unforgetable moments.

To you for reading this book.

Richard Partington
2001

Contents

Wrexham FC, 1973–74. Back row (L–R): M. C. Sutton, G. Davis, R. W. Scott, R. Mostyn, D. P. Smallman. Middle row (L–R): W. Ashcroft, A. G. Hill, H. P. Jones, B. W. Lloyd, T. Vansittart, D. Frogg, J. P. Jones. Front row (L–R): G. Whittle, B. Tinnion, I. Moir, E. C. May, A. T. Griffiths, M. R. Thomas, M. G. Evans.

INTRODUCTION

Wrexham FC are, without any doubt, British football's greatest modern giant-killers. This book relives Wrexham's remarkable exploits and celebrates the significant contribution which the north Wales club and its supporters have made to the excitement, fantasy and magic that is cup football. After all, what is the magic of the cup? It is seldom to be found in all those stale semis and fear-filled finals. The romance of the cup is to be discovered in the journey, not the destination. It is in those lay-bys where the minnows take on the mighty and, against all odds and in defiance of all sporting logic, the underdogs bite their pedigree opponents — and the name of a 'giant killer' enters football folklore.

The seeds of this book were sown back in January 1998. Two events, I think, shaped my thoughts: I had just finished reading Nick Hornby's excellent book *Fever Pitch*; and I had just watched Wrexham playing Premiership Wimbledon in the FA Cup third round replay. Every player in a red shirt was a hero that night and the fans, too, were quite literally having their best game of the season. The cup has always brought out the very best in both Wrexham players and supporters. Unfortunately, there was to be no giant killing that rain-swept night at the Racecourse. But the performance, the atmosphere, the occasion were something very special; something very Wrexham. And that 'something very Wrexham' has, on many occasions, been a truly memorable victory. And I, along with thousands of other fans of the rockin' Robins, have been very fortunate to experience and savour them so many times over the past three decades — Sunderland, Newcastle, Tottenham Hotspur, FC Porto, Arsenal, West Ham, to name but a few.

If those giant-killings were pieces of art (and who says that they are not), they would be on display in the British Museum as a unique and irreplaceable collection, a national treasure, an important part of our heritage that should be lovingly preserved forever. A painting or a sculpture can have no greater claim on my heart and soul.

I hope this book shows that you do not necessarily have to be a fan of Manchester United or Arsenal or any other member of the mega-rich-stock-market-listed-wall-to-wall-designer-foreign stars-Premiership PLC to recognise the taste of glory, to be a part of the national headlines as actual news-makers and to stand proudly on top of the football world. So our moments may be brief and our dreams ultimately under-resourced, but that only makes the memories all the more special.

I read recently that NASA had spent millions of dollars on developing a pen which could operate in the zero-gravity environment of space. When faced with the same challenge and significantly less of a budget, the Russians used a pencil. For me, that story said so much about football generally and the tradition and triumph of giant killing specifically, making the best of what you have got against the big boys and making your mark *etc*, *etc* …   But then, there are not many thoughts or conversations where I find myself unable to seamlessly reference in football generally and Wrexham FC specifically.

There was an article in *Match of the Day* magazine which described Wrexham as a club which had never set the world on fire. HA! For Wrexham, the record books show three FA Cup quarter-finals and quarter-final appearances in both the League Cup and, say it with pride, the European Cup Winners Cup — not bad for a small north Wales club.

But that does not even begin to tell the story. Many top-flight teams have been put to the sword by the fire-breathing red dragons since the early 'Seventies. And, while the giant-killings may be the main event news stories, we all know that there is glory in a performance as well as glory in a victory. While it is the wins that history and commentators always remember, Wrexham's reputation as cup-fighters is also built on the rock-solid foundation of a supporting series of thrilling, stylish displays where the giants have been taken to the limit: Hadjuk Split (1972); AS Roma (1984); Real Zaragosa (1986); the unforgettable Anderlecht games (1976); Burnley (1974); Arsenal (1978); West Ham (1992); of course, that Wimbledon game, and many more as well.

As the song goes, 'It ain't what you do, it's the way that you do it'. And that's important. After all, we do not support Wrexham because we expect to win the League, the FA Cup and League Cup every season. We expect to be entertained. We expect our team to wear their red shirts with pride; to go out there and attack with style and imagination; to defend with courage and heart; to play and compete with passion and commitment; and to give our hopes and dreams a good run for their money. Our team may not be a Premiership high flyer — yet, but they've set my horizons ablaze on many occasions and they've consistently torched the cup ambitions of many giants.

In 1974, Reds' manager John Neal summed up what had been so special about Wrexham's performances after the club's first giant killing run. 'In recent years, giant-killers in the FA Cup have been successful by adopting defensive methods and not allowing the superior opposition to play footbal,' he said. 'The players of Wrexham played very attractive and enterprising football and made many new friends.' These words remain just as true today after 25 years of giant killing.

I hope that you enjoy the memories. Here's to the next magical moments — COME ON YOU REDS!

SOUTHAMPTON v WREXHAM
FA CUP, FIFTH ROUND
Saturday, 16 February, 1974

'You sometimes get a feeling about a club. It's like that with Wrexham. Do not ask me to explain but I cannot help feeling they're about to do some damage in the FA Cup'. Mike Ellis wrote these words in *The Sun* on the eve of the third round of the FA Cup in 1974. And this turned out to be a prediction worthy of Nostradamus, not just for Wrexham's memorable ground-breaking cup run that season, but for their thrilling adventures over the next three decades and, hopefully, far beyond.

It is easy to forget that before the 1973–74 campaign, Wrexham were definitely not what film director Oliver Stone might describe as natural born giant-killers. The club had no reputation whatsoever as cup-fighters. They had only ever made it into the fourth round of the FA Cup on 4 heady occasions in 1928, 1930, 1957 and 1970. As far as I can tell (I'm not one of life's great researchers), the Robins had only once in their hundred year history beaten a team from the Top Division. That was in 1960 when, in the first year of the Football League Cup competition, Wrexham beat First Division Blackburn Rovers 3 - 1 in a fourth round replay.

In 1973, Wrexham were definitely a team on the up. Manager John Neal, appointed in 1968, had guided the club out of the Fourth Division in 1970 and had taken his brave hearts into Europe for the first time two years later (losing only on the away goals rule to Hadjuk Split after putting out FC Zurich in the first round). Neal had assembled an exciting team with the perfect blend of experience and very promising youth at a cost of only £40,000, which was to launch the club on its most successful decade ever.

It was at this time that my dad took me for my debut Wrexham game at the Racecourse. I can remember everything about this momentous event — everything except the opposition, the scorers, or the result. What I can still recall is sitting in the Yale Stand looking at the amazing technicolor spectacle. We had a small black and white TV in those days and watching football had been a stay-up-late-on-a-Saturday-night treat. But *Match of the Day* was just motorway place names and miniature players in various shades of muddy grey. But on that day, I marvelled at how GREEN the pitch was and the vivid RED shirts and that distinctive CRIMSON stripe down the side of the team's white shorts. The players looked so big — so real. And the noise of the crowd, I had never seen so many people in one place before. I had probably not even seen that many people in my entire life. That was clearly a defining moment for me. I suppose the easiest thing to say would be that it was love at first sight and true love never dies.

But what if my dad had taken me to another ground that fateful day? Say, Sealand Road or the Gay Meadow? Would I have become a lifelong Chester fan or a perennial Shrewsbury river-sider there and then? I just cannot see it. In fact, I wake up at night in a cold, panic-stricken sweat when thoughts like that creep into my sleeping brain cells.

Of course, it was no coincidence that my dad took me to see Wrexham. The Robins were his team. And had been for a long time. There is clearly an argument that says my support for Wrexham was simply a wander along in his footsteps. But I cannot buy into that wholly. My dad has had a lifelong love of the music of Jim Reeves. Had he taken me, through the magic of time and space, to see the smooth crooner live in concert, would I have experienced the 'Racecourse effect' in relation to Mr Reeves? I think not.

I'm sure that some professor with a bizarre name, and an obscenely large research grant, must have analysed the reasons why people attach themselves to a particular team. Unfortunately, I have never seen it. I like to think, though, that Wrexham and me were destined to be together. Wrexham was the town where I was born and we, therefore, had the instinctive force of mother nature bonding us together, fusing us as one forever. Well it was either that or I underestimate the magnetic lure of that red stripe on the shorts.

In fact, so impressed was I with that distinctive stripe that I begged my mum to

sew a strip of red material onto my white football shorts. She did and I felt like a king, a swash-buckling Dave Smallman strolling confidently around the play area ready at any second to lash the ball between the two jumpers. The first time that my kit was washed, my shorts turned pink. But I had found my team and I could not have started to watch them at a better time. The giant-killings were about to begin.

As with many remarkable cup campaigns, the origins were somewhat less than spectacular. The Reds trailed for most of their First Round to

John Neal, Wrexham's manager 1968–77

struggling neighbours Shrewsbury Town and only a fortunate goal from Brian Tinnion 10 minutes from the end secured a replay. A place in the second round was booked after a 1 - 0 win at the Gay Meadow and the bandwagon began to roll as Rotherham were duly demolished 3 - 0 at the Racecourse.

The third round saw Wrexham visiting 'old' Second Division (in the days, remember, when the First Division represented the summit of the Football League and the Premier League was not even a twinkle in Rupert Murdoch's eye) high-flyers Crystal Palace, a side brimming with skill and flair which, under Malcolm Allison's flamboyant management, was heading for the top flight. But it was the Robins who soared that afternoon as two second half goals from Sutton and Smallman clinched a great victory.

It was reported that the devastated Palace manager sat in his office drinking champagne and smoking a fat cigar telling anyone who would listen that the better team had lost. There seemed to be two schools of thought on that: Malcolm Allison's, and the rest of the world's.

And so Wrexham found themselves in the fourth round for only the fifth time in their history and a home tie sent north-east Wales cup-crazy. The Reds' opponents were Middlesborough who were top of the Second Division and were to ultimately win the championship by an emphatic 20 points (these were two points for a win days). Jack Charlton was in his first season of management and his team were typified by his young midfield star, Graeme Souness — tough, aggressive, creative, efficient and very, very effective. The match was billed as 'Wrexham's game of the decade' and a 38th minute goal from future Welsh international Dave Smallman buried the 'Boro and propelled the club into unknown, exciting territory, the fifth round of the FA Cup.

Wrexham's reward was an away tie at Southampton, a team lying in twelfth place in the First Division. If the Reds were to progress further, they were going to have to beat this giant now standing in their path.

On paper, it did not look good. Lawrie McMenemy's Saints had only been beaten once at home all season and that was by Don Revie's all-conquering-no-prisoners-taken Leeds United. But, as the cliché goes, in the cup anything can happen. And there was a good omen for the Welsh side, they were to wear their all-white kit, the same colour as … Leeds United (well, if an omen seems good, you grab it). This kit will be known forever by Wrexham fans as the 'lucky white' kit. The team made its first appearance in white at Crystal Palace. Both the Robins' first kit — red — and change kit — blue — clashed with Palace's stripes. A few unsuccessful phone calls around local clubs to borrow a suitable kit resulted in the club forking out for the new white strip and the rest, as they say, is fish and chip wrappers.

But it was more than just a belief in superstition that convinced 60 coaches and three planes packed with Wrexham fans to head for the south coast. The fans

Brian Lloyd thwarts another Southampton attack. [Wrexham Leader]

believed completely in John Neal and his team. It was not through luck that Wrexham had beaten the pretty Palace and the Middlesborough machine. They were deserved victories. Home and away Wrexham had proved to themselves, and to everyone else who cared to take an interest, that they were a match for anyone. Wrexham would not be going into this uncharted territory as carefree tourists content just to enjoy the view. We went there believing we could win.

There was a fantastic atmosphere inside the packed Dell with Wrexham's red and white supporters out-singing their red and white English hosts. The first half saw a very even battle on a heavy pitch with clear-cut chances few and far between. Whittle worked tirelessly in midfield with Tinnion always looking threatening on the right wing. Arfon Griffiths was simply everywhere. At the back, the defensive rock of 6' 3" Eddie May alongside youngsters Joey Jones and Dave Fogg restricted the opportunities for Mike Channon and Co. The best chance of the half fell to Tinnion whose low shot towards the Saints' goal seemed more mud than ball and keeper Martin gratefully saved.

At half-time, the score was 0 - 0. Wrexham's cup dreams were still very much alive. If that scoreline had been offered as the final result to the Welsh masses, it is a sure bet that the instantaneous reply would have been 'thanks — see you at the Racecourse on Tuesday'. But there was to be no need for a replay.

As the second half began, the pattern of play was maintained with Southampton continuing to plug away in midfield and Wrexham launching dangerous counter-attacks. The condition of the pitch was deteriorating all the time, making flowing football almost impossible to play. But both teams tried to entertain and they were producing an enthralling encounter. Then, in the 55th minute, Wrexham won a corner and, as the away fans gave their traditional roar, Tinnion jogged over to the right wing corner flag to launch the ball into the Saints' penalty area. Wrexham were renowned for their dangerous set-pieces. The decisive goals against both Palace and Middlesborough had resulted from Tinnion corners. The winger stepped up and drove over another inch-perfect cross towards the penalty spot. The green-shirted Martin dashed from his line to fist the ball away. Before he could make his clearance, however, David Smallman leapt out of the sapping mud, high into the air, to flash a wonderful header into the Southampton net. 1 - 0!

The 20 year old dark-haired destroyer, with his trademark white sock tassels flapping, saluted the ecstatic Reds' fans as his celebrating team-mates surrounded him. 'Budgie's corner came over', recalled the modest striker who John Neal described as a genius, 'and I just met it with a good header and it flew in'.

For the next 35 minutes of normal play and 4 hour-like minutes of injury time, Wrexham had to survive an onslaught from the wounded First Division side. A combination of some narrow escapes, brilliant defending and superb goalkeeping from Brian Lloyd (who went into the game having not conceded an FA Cup goal for 335 minutes) kept the muddy white shirts ahead of the muddy striped shirts.

As time slipped away from the giants, the Saints' attacks became more desperate. From a long ball into the Wrexham penalty area, Lloyd, a £2,000 bargain buy from Southend, punched clear. Southampton quickly recycled the ball in midfield and fed Paine out wide. He fired in a menacing cross which the defence were unable to clear. The ball broke loose to Gilchrist nine yards out and an equaliser seemed to be his for the taking. Lloyd dashed out and hurled himself as the striker looked up and volleyed. It was the perfect strike. Lloyd instinctively thrust out his hand and miraculously managed to push the ball up and against the crossbar. The ball clattered off the white woodwork, down into the muddy goalmouth and Joey Jones hacked the ball away to safety. Welsh heartbeats restarted shortly afterwards!

When you ask a football lover what is the greatest save ever made by a goalkeeper, many will say it was Gordon Banks' sensational dive to keep out Pele's 1970 power header; others will point to Sunderland's Jim Montgomery's phenomenal FA Cup final double save in 1973. A wider television audience is the only difference between their efforts and Brian Lloyd's heroic point-blank save which propelled Wrexham into the quarter-finals of the FA Cup for the first time as the Saints went marching out. At the final whistle, there were incredible emotional scenes both on and off the pitch as players and supporters realised what had been achieved. The first time only comes once.

The whole of north Wales toasted the mighty Reds (or, more precisely, Whites) and the football world hailed the new giant-killers, WREXHAM. Southampton manager Lawrie McMenemy was generous in his praise of the Third Division side who had given him a 'most miserable afternoon'. But the cup was to give him fonder memories when, just two years later, his side, themselves underdogs, beat Manchester United ('Stokes —1 - 0!') in the final.

'Welcome to Wrexham, the giant-killers,' Burnley manager Jimmy Adamson wrote in his programme notes before the quarter-final clash at Turf Moor on 9 March 1974. The FA Cup draw had presented Wrexham with another away tie at another First Division giant. It is said that there were over 20,000 Wrexham fans in the capacity crowd of 36,000 and they, along with most alleged experts believed that the claret and blues were going to crash out to the white-shirted Welsh wonders. Perhaps if the inspirational Arfon Griffiths, only 6 yards out, had found the net instead of goalkeeper Alan Stevenson's legs after sending him the wrong way, things might have been very different. As it was Wrexham gave their all and though, not at their best, deserved at least a replay.

But that counts for nothing in the cup. When Burnley's Frank Casper collected the ball in midfield, there seemed no real danger. As Dave Fogg moved in to close him down, Casper shot hopefully at goal. The ball struck Fogg's outstretched boot

and looped over the stranded, helpless figure of Lloyd and into the net. 1 - 0. It was a mortal wound; a cruel and unjustified end. The dream was over. There was no disgrace in defeat. We had come such a long way, further than we could ever have imagined back in the winter of 1973. I suppose that, somewhere deep inside, we knew that the adventure had to end. However, I understood that Christmas, birthdays and school holidays had a finite length but it never stopped me hoping.

The muddy 'General' leaves the pitch to be congratulated by the Southampton manager, Lawrie McMenemy. [Wrexham Leader]

There is a parallel universe which we all love to visit occasionally where all the 'if onlys' and 'could have beens' of life become tantalisingly real for a few brief seconds. There, it was so easy to see Griffiths' shot — as it would 99 times out of 100 — give Stevenson no chance and Fogg close down Casper and Wrexham march on proudly to the semi-final and then on to take their rightful place in the 1974 Cup Final. Of course, every supporter of every club lives briefly in that alternative world and breathes its sweet air and analyses that other fate. In these fantasy lands, our teams get the 'rub' and we can almost touch that gleaming silverware.

The truth is, though, that most of us never get to plant that metaphorical kiss on the cold cherished metal. Hundreds of teams set out on the road to Wembley each year and only one can walk the final steps with a big smile. There is nothing more exhilarating or more devastating than the reality of cup football. One mistake, one misjudgement, one moment of magic, one refereeing decision, one piece of sheer bad luck and the journey's over for another year. Wrexham found that there was only heartbreak at the end of their yellow brick road.

The season ended with Wrexham narrowly missing out on promotion to the Second Division. But, after some 100 years, it was clear that Wrexham had finally arrived. A Third Division team of spirit and style had captured, not just their own supporters', but the country's imagination.

A proud giant-killing reputation had been born.

SOUTHAMPTON 0 v 1 WREXHAM
Venue: The Dell
Attendance: 24,797

SOUTHAMPTON:
Eric Martin, Bob McCarthy, Steve Mills, Hugh Fisher, Paul Bennett, Jim Steele, Terry Paine, Mike Channon, Paul Gilchrist, Tony Byrne (Gerry O'Brien), Bobby Stokes
Manager: Lawrie McMenemy

WREXHAM:
Brian Lloyd, Joey Jones, Eddie May, Mickey Evans, David Fogg, Brian Tinnion, Mel Sutton, Arfon Griffiths, Graham Whittle, Geoff Davies, David Smallman
Manager: John Neal
Scorer: Smallman

Referee: D. Turner

WREXHAM v LEICESTER CITY
FOOTBALL LEAGUE CUP, 2ND ROUND
Wednesday, 1 September, 1976

It seems unbelievable, looking back, that the Wrexham heroes who had taken us on that quarter-final odyssey in 1974 and then on to the surreal heights of the European Cup Winners Cup quarter-final in 1976 were still a Third Division side as we entered the seventh season of the decade.

For some bizarre reason, Wrexham have a tradition of being slow-starters to each bright new shiny season, more like Agatha Christie than Linford Christie in racing out of the fixture blocks. For that reason alone, it is not surprising that the club's romance with the League Cup in all its many sponsored guises has generally been more of an occasional but highly memorable one-night late summer stand than a serious deeply-meaningful long-term relationship.

The 1976–77 season, however, was one of a few limited edition collector's item exceptions for, after seeing off Port Vale 2 - 1 on aggregate in the first round, two First Division giants were to fall to the Reds.

John Neal was under no illusions about the size of the task facing his underdogs in the second round as he described Leicester City as 'one of the best footballing sides in the First Division … a side packed with talent'. His analysis was never wide of the mark. City had a proven track record as both a good league and cup side. The previous season, they had lost only ten First Division games and had finished in seventh position. Many pundits expected them to be challenging even harder this time for a place in Europe. This was not surprising because, while the spotlight may have been on their master showman Frank Worthington, the Foxes' team comprised of four full England internationals, with six other players capped at under-23 level.

The season was in its infancy with both teams still finding their feet. In the League, Wrexham had won at home to Portsmouth and lost at Swindon. During these games, however, it had become very clear to Reds' fans that John Neal's new signings were an excellent investment for the club. They were Welsh international centre-half John Roberts and former Walsall and Cambridge striker Bobby Shinton. It was certainly too early in the fixture list to talk about cup fever, but there was certainly an expectant buzz around the Racecourse as the game got underway with the Reds kicking into the Kop end. Cup nights in Wrexham had become very special occasions and we did not expect our team to lose. In fact, more than that, we expected our team to win, and win playing the most exhilarating, attacking football imaginable. We were not about to be disappointed.

From the first whistle, Wrexham surged forward with Griffiths and Thomas taking a tight grip of the midfield. Both men went close to opening the scoring in the first 15 minutes as blue shirts chased red shadows. But the classy Foxes weathered the early storm and began to find the menacing Worthington upfront. Only a stunning save from the ever-reliable Lloyd stopped Chris Garland from giving the visitors' an unwelcome lead with virtually their first serious attack of the game.

Wrexham heeded the warning. But their game plan was not, and could never be, cautious defence. The Reds continued to play the positive football, with the twin towers of Roberts and Davis keeping a watchful eye on Mr Worthington. Shinton came close to breaking the deadlock when he was found in space in City's penalty area, only to blaze a shot over Wallington's bar into the packed masses on the Kop.

Leicester may have had a reputation as a cultured football team, but they were not averse to some crude tackling as they found themselves outplayed and outclassed by the Third Division side. First, Blockley crunched in on the ever-dangerous Shinton and, then, Alderson for once managed to catch up with the lively Thomas and dispatched him to the lush turf.

At half-time, it was goalless and there can be no doubt that it was the First Division side who would have been the happiest with that scoreline. Wrexham had played the better football and created the most chances, but with 45 minutes to go and the sides still level, that meant nothing.

As I sat with my dad in the Yale Stand, we expected the First Division side to come out for the second half, awakened by Wrexham's warning shots, firing on all cylinders. But it was our own team who again grasped the initiative with the solid figure of Mel Sutton driving in a number of excellent crosses into the Leicester penalty area. From one centre, Reds' target man Billy Ashcroft rose high into the night sky to power a header which Wallington scrambled to save at the foot of his post. But it was not to be all one-way traffic. In the 52nd minute, Wrexham conceded a free-kick just outside their penalty area. Frank Worthington rubbed his hands. I sunk back into my red plastic seat and half-closed my eyes hardly daring to look. Worthington, who had only been allowed to display brief flashes of the magic which he was clearly capable of, lined up behind the ball. Lloyd anxiously marshalled the red wall into position. Then, with the whistle, Worthington ran in and arced a brilliant drive at goal which Lloyd tipped around the post for a corner. Three sides of the ground cheered their hero in a green shirt.

This was not, however, the spark for a major Leicester offensive as it only spurred Wrexham on to take an even tighter grip of the game. Griffiths, Thomas and Sutton overwhelmed the midfield and, with Shinton and Ashcroft up-front always

Gareth Davis, the Wrexham captain.

looking threatening, it looked like Wrexham would take the lead at any time. The First Division Foxes really began to buckle under the intense and almost unrelenting pressure from the home side, but that vital goal would not come. It looked like Shinton had made the breakthrough at one point as he raced on to beat the advancing Wallington to a driven cross on the edge of the six-yard box. We leapt out of our seats screaming with delight as the ball passed Wallington on its way towards goal, only to see his left foot shot cannon against the Tech end crossbar. I sank back again into the hard plastic seat. Was that to be our luck tonight?

Everything about the Reds' display had been superb. Leicester were one of the best footballing sides in the country and they were run ragged. But, as this great game entered its final minutes, the two teams were staring at a replay. Leicester had certainly given up on any aspiration to even get near the Wrexham goal and sought to pack out their defence.

Finally, Wrexham's excellent display was crowned with the goal that it deserved, and it was fitting that the providers were the stars of the night, the smallest players on the pitch, Griffiths and Thomas. A short corner exchange between the two players caught the City defence flat footed. Griffiths chipped in a neat centre and, while all eyes looked for the imposing figure of big Billy Ashcroft, captain Gareth Davis took command to direct his header past Wallington's despairing dive and the ball was in the net. 1 - 0.

The crowd went wild with a mixture of triumph and relief. Davis who had, all night, quietly gone about his business of keeping the spectacular Worthington under wraps, was mobbed by red shirts. 'I suddenly found myself in my favourite scoring position — two yards out,' said the Reds' skipper. 'I never miss from there'.

Vital last-minute cup goals were to be something of a speciality for Gareth Davis. I can remember him sending my heart into orbit with his vital second goal against Djurgardens in the second round of the Cup Winners Cup in 1975; the equaliser at home to Spurs in 1979 to send the third round replay into extra time; and the equaliser at Upton Park in 1981 to bring the cup holders back to Wales for a victorious third round replay. He was a true captain who, from the back, led from the front.

It was a killer blow for the First Division side. There was still time for the Foxes, but Wrexham continued to hunt them. The red shirts had worked too hard to throw their advantage away. And then it was all over. Wrexham had won, First Division Leicester City were out, and the Robins' reputation as giant-killers was confirmed once again.

My dad drove us home and we talked about a captain doing a captain's thing, and about who we would like in the third round. We had fish and chips and they tasted good because the salt and vinegar of life was just right! 'Everything was so good tonight,' purred John Neal after the game. 'Perfect pitch, lovely night for football, big opposition … and a tremendous result'.

WREXHAM 1 v 0 LEICESTER CITY
Venue: The Racecourse
Attendance: 9,776

WREXHAM:
Brian Lloyd, Mickey Evans, Alan Dwyer, Gareth Davis, John Roberts, Mike Thomas, Bobby Shinton (Graham Whittle), Mel Sutton, Billy Ashcroft, Stuart Lee, Arfon Griffiths
Manager: John Neal
Scorer: Davis

LEICESTER CITY:
Mark Wallington, Steve Whitworth, Dennis Rofe, Steve Kimber, Jeff Blockley, Allan Woollett, Keith Birchenall, Frank Worthington, Bob Lee, Chris Garland
Manager: Jimmy Bloomfield

Referee: J. Taylor

TOTTENHAM HOTSPUR v WREXHAM
FOOTBALL LEAGUE CUP, 3RD ROUND
Wednesday, 22 September, 1976

Wrexham's reward for their League Cup giant-killing was an away tie against another First Division giant Tottenham Hotspur. 'It's a great honour and another tremendous challenge', confirmed the Reds' secretary, Norman Wilson. 'We would have preferred them here at home at Wrexham, but we have got a job to do and we will go down there to do it'. And what a job the team did. While there had been that tremendous run to the FA Cup quarter-final, few would argue that the finest display in the club's history up to that time, happened at White Hart Lane as Spurs, a team forever known for its flair and creativity (and terrible FA Cup songs), were given the most comprehensive footballing lesson that fine London night.

It would be wrong to portray Wrexham as a run-of-the-mill Third Division outfit. They were no ordinary underdogs with four full Welsh internationals in their starting line-up: Brian Lloyd, John Roberts, Mickey Thomas and Arfon Griffiths, and the Robins' dynamic front trio of Whittle, Shinton and Ashcroft destroyed defences for fun and, between them, were to plunder an incredible 81 league and cup goals during the season. But, for this cup-tie, Wrexham were very much the underdogs.

This was the first meeting between the two sides and it was not a good time for Spurs to make the Welsh club's acquaintance. The London side had not made the best of starts to their campaign having taken only five points from their first six games and pressure on their manager, Keith Burkinshaw, was already mounting. Going into this important cup-tie, his message to his team had been 'football of quality in midfield is futile unless backed up by aggression and thrust in the goalmouth'. Unfortunately for him, it was Wrexham who practised what he preached.

After an initial flourish from the white shirts, Wrexham soon began to play the better and more incisive football. It must have seemed unbelievable to the 19,000 supporters watching that the team in red shirts was from a lower division — and only in fourth place! That night at least, there were definitely not three teams better than Wrexham in the whole of the Football League as the giant-killing machine, powered on by the sleek turbo-engine of Griffiths, Thomas and Sutton, dominated the first half. A spectacular 30-yard left-footed drive from Thomas was well-saved by Jennings who was probably the best keeper in the world at that time. From the

Jennings watches the ball sailing into the roof of the net. [Wrexham Leader]

resulting Shinton corner, Ashcroft steered a header close to the target. Soon after, Whittle lashed a 20 yard drive at goal which Jennings again clawed away.

The young Spurs midfield maestro, Glenn Hoddle, and the ever-green Ralph Coates were left looking lost and lonely as their game plan was cut to ribbons by the flying Robins. Hoddle and friends must have wondered what they had done in a previous life to deserve this kind of a nightmare. Shinton down the right; Thomas down the left; Whittle and big Billy Ashcroft causing chaos through the centre. Pat Jennings' huge hands were called into action on numerous occasions to keep his stuttering side on level terms. A goal seemed imminent at any moment.

It duly arrived after 36 minutes. The artful Shinton broke clear, Jennings raced out and drove the bearded striker wide. Shinton still fired in his shot but it was blocked. The ball rebounded kindly back to the Wrexham man. He looked up and saw Thomas arriving like the proverbial red express train. Shinton crossed and the little Welshman whipped a left foot shot into the roof of the net. 1 - 0.

Just over five minutes later, Wrexham doubled their lead as the silky skills of Shinton unlocked the home defence once more as he found Thomas in space. The incoming Naylor tried to intercept but Thomas was not to be shaken off the ball and

Ashcroft makes the score 3 - 0 at White Hart Lane. [Wrexham Leader]

he rifled another quality finish low past Jennings into the net. 2 - 0.

The Londoners were unable to find questions let alone answers to Wrexham's energy, skill and pace and only two further excellent saves by the tall Irishman and a goal-line clearance by Naylor saved them from a humiliating rout. At half-time, at 0 - 2 down, there must have been some consolation for the home fans that the scoreline was not much worse and things probably could not get any worse.

A few minutes into the second half, life indeed got worse for the First Division side. Shinton was again the creator, spotting Ashcroft's run through the shell-shocked defence, and finding him with a perfectly weighted pass from the right. Ashcroft coolly took the ball in his stride and curled a brilliant shot into the Spurs net. 3 - 0, 3 - 0!

An amazing three goal lead at White Hart Lane to the Third Division heroes! And, do not forget, these were the days when the giants still put out their first teams in the early rounds of the League Cup. At this point, I am convinced that the Reds eased down a couple of gears to give Jennings' back a rest and the white shirts a chance to play with the ball — it was theirs after all. Coates was replaced by the lively John Pratt and the substitute injected some life into the wounded giants. In the 55th minute, Lloyd fisted away Neighbour's swinging corner, the ball fell to Hoddle about 25 yards and he crashed an unstoppable drive through the crowded penalty area, possibly taking a deflection, on its way past the startled Reds' keeper into the net. 3 - 1.

Eight minutes later, the Spurs revival continued. A sweeping move involving Pratt, Perryman, Hoddle and Jones stretched the Reds and Moores capitalised on a moment's generosity in the Wrexham penalty area to scramble another goal from close range. 3 - 2

The home crowd's lost cause had suddenly been found, along with their voices and they roared their team on in pursuit of salvation. But Wrexham did not surrender. While they were not able to rediscover fully their earlier scintillating form, they never looked like losing the game. Davis and Roberts remained composed in the heart of the defence and full-backs Evans and Dwyer were reliable sentries on the flanks. Upfront, the Reds' strikeforce continued to expose the vulnerability of the Spurs backline and only yet another fingertip save over the bar from Jennings kept out a trademark Whittle missile.

As it was, no further goals were scored and, at the final whistle, the 1,000 plus Wrexham fans celebrated a superb performance and another famous victory. As in the last round, the one-goal margin flattered the giants. John Neal hailed 'the best display since I've been manager — and that's saying a lot'. Pat Jennings reflected sadly, 'a team of our experience should have beaten a side from a lower division. But the first thing we must do against sides like Wrexham is to match them for effort. This we failed to do from the start'.

Wrexham's League Cup campaign came to a crashing halt in the Midlands in the next round when they were beaten 5 - 1 (five lucky breakaways?) by Aston Villa in front of 41,000 at Villa Park. A certain centre forward named Andy Gray was the main destroyer, scoring two goals and giving the Reds' defence a torrid night. Mr Gray may have forgotten all about that evening but I've never subscribed to *Sky Sports*!

That was one of the very rare occasions that the 'giant-killers' failed to do themselves justice against top-class opponents. But that future cloud should not be allowed to cast a shadow over the dazzling display at White Hart Lane that September night. Admiring the Reds at White Hart Lane was the Crystal Palace, and future England, manager Terry Venables who observed that Wrexham's display was 'the most outstanding performance I have seen from any team this season. They completely outplayed Spurs'.

And there was still room left in the season for a little bit more cup glory.

TOTTENHAM HOTSPUR 2 v 3 WREXHAM
Venue: White Hart Lane
Attendance: 19,156

TOTTENHAM HOTSPUR:
Pat Jennings, Terry Naylor, Don McAllister, Glenn Hoddle, Willie Young, Keith Osgood, Ralph Coates (John Pratt), Steve Perryman, Ian Moores, Chris Moores, Jimmy Neighbour
Manager: Keith Burkinshaw
Scorers: Hoddle, Moores

WREXHAM:
Brian Lloyd, Mickey Evans, Alan Dwyer, Gareth Davis, John Roberts, Mike Thomas, Bobby Shinton, Mel Sutton, Billy Ashcroft, Graham Whittle, Arfon Griffiths
Manager: John Neal
Scorers: Thomas (2), Ashcroft (1)

Referee: R. Challis

WREXHAM v SUNDERLAND
FA CUP, 3RD ROUND REPLAY
Wednesday, 12 January, 1977

There were never very many football terrace songs that I could sing at our kitchen table which would not have sent the tea spraying out of my mum and dad's mouths. 'Six foot two, eyes of blue, big Jim Holton's after you' had long been one that I could happily warble without fear of a Tetley ejaculation. The third round draw served up a clash of the titans with the aforesung big Jim Holton of Sunderland facing up to Wrexham's flame-haired striker big Billy Ashcroft.

However, as is the way, the side that already taken on and beaten two First Division giants that season and who, months earlier, had given Mr Rensenbrink and his Anderlecht mates such a tough time in the European Cup Winners Cup quarter-final, needed a replay against non-league Goole Town to scrape through into the second round. A much more convincing performance followed as Chesterfield were dispatched 6 - 0 at the Racecourse and Wrexham were rewarded with a tie at the 1973 FA Cup winners.

In the Roker Park furnace, Wrexham went 2 - 0 ahead in front of a fanatical 23,356 crowd with, first, Ashcroft hooking a right foot drive on the turn into the home side's goal, and then Graham Whittle scoring one of the great goals. The Reds' number ten received the ball in midfield and, as Holton moved in, the talented Liverpudlian dropped his shoulder, sent the tall defender the wrong way, and then launched an unstoppable 25-yard pile-driver into the top corner of the Sunderland net. Many of the goals that Wrexham fans remember from the 'Seventies were scored by Graham Whittle and his match-winning, match-changing, firepower. Fierce, blistering drives from 20, 30, 40 yards out, left foot or right, they were Whittle's trademark. OK, maybe the years colour the memories, but I know that his goals were spectacular. And I also know that if Whittle had been born in Brazil and playing *circa* 1970, they would still be showing his goals on TV today. John Neal was not wrong when he said that it was a 'tragedy that Graham Whittle never got the chance of playing in the First Division'. But the even bigger tragedy was that injury forced Whittle to retire from the game in his late 20s.

Billy Ashcroft.
[Wrexham Leader]

But Whittle's and Ashcroft's goals were not enough to produce a giant-killing at the first time of asking. The famous Roker roar seemed to come to the home side's rescue as the red and white stripes were inspired to claw their way back onto level terms. In the final few minutes, it was the white shirts of Wrexham who had to cling on for a replay as they had to finish the game with ten men after Ashcroft was carried off with an injury,

And so there was to be a midweek replay at the Racecourse. These were the days when replays took place only some 48 to 72 hours after the first game and you really felt swept breathlessly along on the momentum of a cup run. Stand tickets were quickly snapped up. There was yet another outbreak of cup fever in north Wales; the symptoms were by now well-known. John Neal, however, was quick to prescribe a strong dose of realism. 'Despite Sunderland's low League position at the moment, they are still one of the biggest clubs in the land, and a First Division side'.

Sunderland were facing almost certain relegation from the top division. But that only made success in the FA Cup all the more vital to their loyal fans. The club had

Graham Whittle.
[Wrexham Leader]

invested big money both for the time and certainly in comparison to Wrexham's modest investments, on trying to cement their short-term future to soccer's summit. Three key purchases had been goalkeeper Barry Siddall from Bolton for £60,000, the aforesung big Jim Holton from Manchester United for £80,000 and striker Bob Lee, a £200,000 buy from Leicester City.

If Mr Lee was going to compile his personal list of 'football grounds where I love to play', it is a reasonable bet that the Racecourse would be unlikely to feature too highly in his top 92 — he had first hand experience of Wrexham's giant-killing capabilities earlier in the season when he wore the blue of Leicester. For all their past might and glory and current portfolio of talent and ambition, Sunderland were a struggling side. They had lost their last seven games and had failed to score a single League goal. When you are on a run like that, probably the last team you want to find in your path is Third Division Wrexham.

It was a bitterly cold night in north Wales with a light skimmering of soft snow on the pitch. But half-an-hour before the kick-off, the atmosphere inside the ground was already close to boiling point. If I had to give my very own 'Oscar' for Best Away Fans in a Supporting Role at the Racecourse, there would be no doubt in my mind about the winners, Sunderland. Their red-blooded passion and pride in their team, their humour, their awesome intensity and noise was tremendous to watch and hear and always brought out the best in the home fans who took up the challenge. And that night was one of the best atmospheres that I had ever experienced as Wrexham's Kop took on and, aided by the sheer brilliance and inspiration of their team, defeated the Roker roar.

As my dad and I clambered up the rear of the Kop, we were faced by a solid mass of home supporters. We made our way along towards the centre. Through this almost solid wall of coated, scarved and hatted backs, I was just able to steal the occasional, tantalising glimpse of the sacred turf, its white dusting sparkling in the floodlit night. Soon, we were at the foot of the 'pigeon loft', the stand the club had bought from one of the town's long ago closed-down and demolished cinemas and relocated, like a half-open clam, above the concrete terracing. There was a quick conversation between my dad and a man standing by the door and then suddenly we were climbing dark steps; a stairway to heaven as far as I was concerned, for what lay at the top were seats (very uncomfortable seats actually, but I did not care) which gave me the most perfect view. I had not realised at the time, but my dad had paid for a transfer from the ground as he knew that the chances of me seeing much of the game from the packed Kop were about as good as The Osmonds doing a duet with the Sex Pistols. I looked around from my nest. The stadium was already packed. The noise of the Kop rose up and surrounded us. The chants from the Sunderland fans at the far end tried to invade our territory. As the time drew closer and closer to 7.30, the vocal battle just got louder and more intense.

Obviously, I did not know it at the time but this was to be my one and only appearance in the 'pigeon loft' (health and safety regulations were soon to force its closure). And it was to be truly memorable. I would like to say that it was because of the result and the performance. But, for most of the game, my over-riding emotion was one of dread. As the Reds finally ran out onto the pitch, I was convinced that someone had launched an Apollo rocket under the stand. Sure there was the noise, but everyone below seemed to be banging the sides of this rather flimsy structure and, to my amazement and horror, everyone seated around me seemed to be stamping their feet. It seemed to me that at any cataclysmic moment, this rickety four-legged beast would buckle and fall. I had been used to the relative luxury and modern concrete assurance of the Yale Stand. I was only ten years old. As the green shirt of Brian Lloyd ran towards us applauding, I concluded that toys were nice, but I would have been wiser asking for a parachute as a Christmas present.

As the game got underway in this cauldron of noise and shaking architecture, Wrexham showed that they were not suffering from any hangover from their Roker near miss as, kicking towards us, they forced six corners in the first quarter-of-an-hour. Sunderland's defence looked decidedly stressed as Shinton, Whittle and the fully-recovered Ashcroft provided a potent, razor sharp spearhead.

The yellow shirts of the First Division side were barely in the game as the Reds launched attack after attack without quite creating that killer opening. In the 28th minute, the wily Arfon Griffiths sent over a quick freekick and Whittle was the first to react, sending a fierce header inches off target. The crowd roared and the stand shook again. I was prepared, I had decided, to risk life and limb if a goal was scored, but to raise my, and thousands of others, expectations with a narrow miss was nothing, I thought, but irresponsible as I clung on to the back of the quaking seat in front of me.

The game came to an abrupt halt soon after, when left-back Alan Dwyer fell awkwardly, dislocating his shoulder, and had to be helped from the pitch. Wrexham had to reorganise their defence. Substitute Wayne Ciegelski came on and went into the centre of defence alongside John Roberts. Gareth Davis moved across to right-back and the versatile and ever-dependable Mickey Evans switched over to the left.

The injury and the changes seemed to break Wrexham's rhythm and for the remainder of the half, they were not quite able to recover their earlier drive and fluency. But they were still immeasurably better than their First Division opponents. And I know that we should have had a penalty. From a right-wing corner, big Billy Ashcroft rose on the edge of the six-yard box. A yellow-shirted arm blatantly pushed him forwards. I saw it clearly. Ashcroft's back arched as he vainly tried to reach the ball. The Kop, well those like me with a clear view from right behind the goal, screamed 'PENALTY!' and howled in disbelief as the referee failed to react and Sunderland escaped justice. At half-time, the game was goalless. Wrexham had dominated the play, but the First Division giants were still very much alive and kicking.

Sunderland began the second half much brighter and, almost immediately, Holden directed a header at Lloyd. This seemed to stir my mighty Reds into life and, while Shinton was receiving treatment on the touchline following a foul by Bolton, they cut effortlessly through Sunderland's defence and Whittle fired in a low drive which Siddall dived to save. With Shinton's return to the action, Wrexham took hold of this gripping cup tie. But for all of the Reds' controlled man-to-man passing and, at times, mesmerising skills, the breakthrough would not come.

And then in the 63rd minute, winter became summer. And it was good old 'Route One' football, mixed with a little bit of magic. From Lloyd's long clearance, the whole Sunderland defence was caught square and Reds' flame-haired target man big Billy Ashcroft found himself in space with the ball at his feet. Big Jim Holton, who had been engaged in a virtually non-stop war of attrition with the Reds' battling striker for over 150 minutes of 'no prisoners' cup action, raced over to cover. But big Billy turned him inside and out with the skill and speed of George Best at, well, his best, and then with the space he had created, crashed an unstoppable low shot past Siddall into the net. 1 - 0.

For the first time in the match, the far Tech end was motionless and, I guess, silent. I could not tell if they were quiet or not because I was above, within, a volcanic Kop. It was big Billy's 16th goal of the season and he would never score a better one. I knew that I would always be able to picture his strike as my seat swayed and rattled and groaned in the delirious bedlam. Of course, I was now an integral part of this wild, euphoric, earthquake and even felt brave enough to stamp my feet a couple of times.

We had the lead. We deserved the lead. Now we had to preserve the lead. The rest of the game proved to be very enjoyable. Having survived the celebratory explosion, I began to have as much confidence in this unique structure as I had in the defensive pillars of Davis, Roberts, Ciegelski and Evans. In the final minutes of the game, John Neal even moved Ashcroft back to bolster the Reds' aerial defences. There was only one scare really when Kerr broke down the right wing and found Clarke in space. But the striker wasted his chance and, despite the ravenous roars of the Roker refugees, Sunderland were a beaten team and they seemed to know it long before the referee blew the final whistle. Saturday's escape tunnel had caved in.

It was the Racecourse roar that lasted long into that cold night. As we made our way down the steps, I resisted any urge to kneel down and kiss the concrete. Wrexham had won, another giant-killing. I was back on solid ground. All was well with my universe.

'Justice was done on the night,' said John Neal after the game. 'It was a terrific cup tie. The lads did me proud tonight. I've lost count of the number of times I've said that. What big hearts they all have. It's amazing what that, coupled with skill, has achieved'. And big Billy Ashcroft had won the clash of the titans. 'This Ashcroft is a good player,' observed Neal, 'better than many people think.'

The fourth round draw sent Wrexham down for a classic Welsh derby with the Pricipality's only Second Division side, Cardiff City. The Reds were below par that day but still managed to come back from 2 - 0 down to seemingly force a replay with a last minute equaliser. Did they relax then thinking that the return match was booked? Did they go out in their open style to try to win the game in those dying seconds? I honestly cannot remember. And, well, it does not really matter. Because the final score was 3 - 2 to Cardiff. And that mattered a lot.

Regrettably, last-minute defeat and disappointment was to become an unfortunate habit that season. What had seemed certain, and thoroughly earned, promotion to the Second Division disintegrated as Wrexham, needing only two points to clinch their little bit of history, lost their last two home games to Crystal Palace (who were to be promoted in the Reds' place) and already-crowned champions Mansfield Town to finish outside of the top three. The Crystal Palace game, in particular, was a real sickener when Wrexham came back from 2 - 0 down to draw level through a Whittle 30-yarder and a John Lyons' header; a draw which would probably have been enough to seal promotion. But Palace had other ideas and scored two devastating injury time goals to win 4 - 2.

It was the bitterest disappointment at the end of what had been a fantastic season. I do not think that football has ever actually made me cry, but it has come very close on a few occasions. This was one of them.

It was to be John Neal's last season in charge at the Racecourse. His success as a manager, personified and advertised by Wrexham's giant killing triumphs, had been noted by many top clubs and First Division Middlesborough made him an offer he could not refuse. Everyone was sad to see him leave, but he deserved success. John Neal had been a wonderful servant and ambassador for the club. He had nurtured and brought on some exciting home-grown young players (Thomas,

Whittle, Smallman, Davis, Jones, Ashcroft, Dwyer, *etc*), brought the best out of Wrexham's seasoned pros (Griffiths, May, Evans, *etc*); and had the instinct and insight to know a bargain buy (Shinton, Sutton, Lloyd, Roberts, *etc*).

My own personal memory of John Neal relates to a junior penalty shoot-out competition organised by the club at their old Stansty training ground. The memory is of four precious words spoken by the Reds' manager to me. 'I like it son,' he said as my first penalty actually sent Wrexham's reserve goalkeeper Eddie Niedzwiecki the wrong way. I scored three out of five — well, I had the club's future to think of. I did not want to undermine the confidence of Wrexham's future number one, it seemed only right to let Eddie save a couple. It was a small sacrifice for a young boy to make to ensure that his team, and indeed his country, would, literally, be in safe hands!

John Neal had taken the club from the Fourth Division to the brink of the Second, built a team renowned for its flair and exciting football, enjoyed quarter-final success in both the FA Cup and European Cup Winners Cup, and established the club as famous giant-killers (three First Division sides beaten during this season alone). John Neal had a special place in the heart of every Wrexham player and fan. He had given us dreams that were real. He had provided the foundation for a reality which was, the next season, to be beyond our wildest dreams. The best was still to come.

WREXHAM 1 v 0 SUNDERLAND
Venue: The Racecourse
Attendance: 16,023

WREXHAM:
Brian Lloyd, Mickey Evans, Alan Dwyer (Wayne Ciegelski), Gareth Davis, John Roberts, Mike Thomas, Bobby Shinton, Mel Sutton, Billy Ashcroft, Graham Whittle, Arfon Griffiths.
Manager: John Neal
Scorer: Ashcroft

SUNDERLAND:
Barry Siddall, Jackie Ashurst, Joe Bolton, Mick Henderson, Jeff Clarke, Jim Holton, Bobby Kerr, Shaun Elliott, Mel Holden, Bob Lee, Gary Rowell (Kevin Arnott)
Manager: Jimmy Adamson

Referee: C. Seel

WREXHAM v BRISTOL CITY
FOOTBALL LEAGUE CUP, 3RD ROUND
Wednesday, 26 October, 1977

The previous season's unprecedented exploits were to be surpassed this year. However, the traditional poor start to the campaign had seemed even more depressing as the club and supporters were still hurting from the previous season's catastrophe. Under the new management of longest serving player, Arfon Griffiths, the Reds' first three Third Division League games had brought only two draws and a defeat. There were rumours of a number of players wanting to get away. There seemed the very really possibility that the critical mass that had been created would implode.

At least, though, having finally developed a taste for the League Cup the previous season, Wrexham kept their seat at the dining table as they managed to struggle past Stockport County in the first round, winning 2 - 1 on aggregate. Big Billy Ashcroft had scored the decisive goal but his former manager rated the striker highly and Ashcroft left for First Division Middlesborough for a fee of £125,000. This did nothing for terrace morale. Griffiths made it clear that he would not be rushed into signing a replacement. 'Now I have the problem of replacing Billy and it's not going to be easy. I have to be sure to get the right one'. And so Wrexham travelled to Second Division Charlton Athletic for the second round tie with Stuart Lee, a player who in his two seasons with the club had never been able to command a regular first team place, stepping into the front line.

This was to be the game that saw Wrexham begin to rediscover their form and self-belief as they tore into their higher league opponents and missed a stack of excellent chances. Then, with just over an hour gone, Charlton took the lead with a controversial penalty. This game proved to the fans, and probably more importantly to the players themselves, that the team still had the character, the belief and the ability to scale the heights as they turned what could have been unjust defeat into deserved victory. A Shinton lob and a late own goal provided the 2 - 1 win at The Valley and, from that point, there was no looking back. Momentum was added to the team's resurgence with the key signings of Welsh international goalkeeper Dai Davies from Everton for £10,000 and, for Ashcroft's replacement, Arfon got the right one, a £60,000 signing from Hereford United who was already a goal-scoring legend in the lower divisions; enter Dixie McNeil. Their signings, along with winger

Les Cartwright's £40,000 transfer from Coventry in pre-season, completed the jigsaw.

The third round draw presented Wrexham with a home tie against Bristol City. Third Division Robins versus First Division Robins. A buzz went around the town; a chance of yet another giant-killing. Winter may have been approaching but now the season was beginning to warm up nicely.

Wrexham's League campaign was now 14 games old going into this third round tie. The Reds were lying in fourth place, level on points (17) with the three teams above them. Bristol City were in their second season in the top-flight, having just avoided relegation the previous year. It was already clear that they were in for another similar battle come next May. Having played 11 games in the League, City were lying fifth from bottom, just above the drop zone, having collected just seven points. But I did not base my assessment of teams by just their League position. I gauged them by the edited highlights on Saturday night's *Match of the Day* and I had seen City's Tom Ritchie score a cracker against Liverpool and I knew they would be dangerous. If City needed any added incentive to win this tie, many of their fellow First Division clubs had already been knocked out of this competition. And some optimistic noises were emanating from Ashton Gate about a great chance to qualify for Europe. And, for the League Cup, Wrexham would have to do without the services of the cup-tied Dixie McNeil.

'We naturally fancy our chances', said Arfon Griffiths before the game. 'We are capable of playing against good opposition and we are looking forward to meeting them ... If we go out, it won't bother me, the League is our priority'.

Most fans expected the experienced Stuart Lee to be recalled to fill Dixie's Nº 9 shirt. But Arfon handed the responsibility to John Lyons, the young Buckley-born striker. In all the games that I saw John Lyons play, he never let us down, he was a truly whole-hearted player who always played with tremendous commitment, passion, determination and enjoyment. We all connected with John Lyons. He was a Wrexham fan who grew up to become a Wrexham player. He was living our dream. In the League, when Dixie was injured, and in the League Cup, John Lyons led the line superbly and I think he was one of the unsung heroes of this great Wrexham side. I can still remember the complete numbing, disbelieving shock when I read the *Evening Leader* headlines of his tragic death a few years later. He had by then moved from Wrexham to pursue his career down south. Things had clearly gone wrong, very wrong for him. At times like that you realise both the unimportance and yet also the relative importance of football. I had never met him, but it felt like the loss of a friend. I will always remember John Lyons rampaging towards goal, always in the thick of the action, a smile never far from his face. The tie against Bristol City is certainly a part of these memories; Lyons along with the other ten men in red shirts was a star.

In the first half, City set out their stall to defend and keep Wrexham entangled in a midfield battle. There were only two real incidents of note. The first, was at the Tech end when Mann's 20-yard drive somehow squirmed through Dai Davies' hands. A few hundred west country fans got as far as the 'OA' of 'GOAL' before the Welsh international flashed around to collect the elusive ball on the line to the accompaniment of relieved cheers from the rest of the ground

At the Kop end, another typical Graham Whittle thunderbolt comprehensibly beat Shaw's outstretched hands. Again, a few thousand home fans got as far as the 'OA' in 'GOAL' in vertical take-off mode. But the 'OA' translated seamlessly and effortlessly into 'OARRR' as the white-shirted Sweeney, strategically placed on the goal line, stood firm to head the ball away. My dismay at the clearance was, I think, overshadowed by my amazement to see Mr Sweeney's head still attached to his shoulders. Even my worst nightmares had never placed my head in the way of a full-blooded Graham Whittle missile.

At half-time, the game was goalless. It was far from a classic. It was clearly going to plan for City. I suppose, looking back, City's approach was a benchmark of their respect for the Third Division giant-killers. Last season had clearly spoilt me. I had been incredibly fortunate to witness not just giant-killings, but pulsating, entertaining cup-ties. The very ordinary 45 minutes that had just passed was not that bad, it just seemed it. 'The first half was even', observed the Wrexham manager later. 'But the second half was only one team — ours'.

Wrexham started the second half two gears higher, determined not to be dragged down by the First Division opposition and we got the ideal start — a goal. Only six minutes had passed when Cartwright played a delicate ball wide out to Whittle on the left wing. Whittle cruised down the touchline towards the Tech end, escorted by a white shirt. With a final burst of acceleration, Whittle evaded any challenge and from the by-line hit a wonderful deep left-foot cross to the far post. There seemed too many white shirts in the penalty area, but as Shaw scrambled across his line, Shinton breezed in from nowhere to power a header past the goalkeeper's diving left-hand into the net. 1 – 0.

Almost before the ball had reached its target, Shinton's run had turned into a celebration. He peeled away, both arms aloft, with John Lyons and John Roberts in hot pursuit, to take his acclaim from the Yale Stand. 'Oh Bobby, Bobby — Bobby, Bobby, Bobby, Bobby Shi-inton' the Kop sang over and over again. The showman applauded his orbiting audience.

Now City could no longer sit back. Their negative approach was now not good enough. They had to come out and play the beautiful game if they wanted to regain their view of Wembley's twin towers. But, though they tried hard, they were given a demonstration in the finer arts as Wrexham dominated for long periods with the dogged Mel Sutton directing the midfield assault. City were completely outclassed

Bobby Shinton and Dixie McNeil.
[Wrexham Leader]

by Wrexham's superior work rate and majestic, clinical passing. It was beautiful to watch; beautifully familiar to watch. Shinton shot over when a pass inside to Whittle would probably have seen the lead doubled. City wanted to be camped in the Wrexham half but they were overpowered and overrun by red shirts. Wrexham attack seemed to follow Wrexham attack. A Whittle shot cracked against the bar and, with nine minutes remaining, Lyons broke clear only to see his shot bounce back off the post.

I am sure that there must have been at least one attack from the First Division side and some nervous moments, but I cannot recall any. It was a comprehensive 1 - 0 thrashing. The final whistle brought another great giant-killing night to a close and Wrexham left the pitch to a standing ovation.

'I thought they were rather lucky to get off with a one goal defeat', commented Arfon Griffiths on his side's masterful performance. 'I don't think anyone in the game was really surprised that we beat Bristol City ... we were tight at the back, compact in midfield, and always looking dangerous up-front'. For the truly impartial assessment of the game, there was Man United's Lou Macari who advised the waiting media that 'Wrexham deserved it without a doubt — they slaughtered them'.

In the fourth round, Wrexham had a tough battle with fellow Third Division outfit Swindon. However, goals from Lyons and Whittle secured the home victory and the prize of a quarter-final tie at the Racecourse against the reigning League and European Champions, Bob Paisley's seemingly-invincible Liverpool. Emlyn Hughes, Liverpool and England captain, paid Wrexham the ultimate compliment. 'As far as I am concerned, this was the hardest draw we could have had. It will be very, very difficult for us ... I'll be happy to settle for a draw and to take Wrexham to Anfield'.

It was a January night to remember at the Racecourse, a fantastic atmosphere to rival the Anderlecht game with over 25,000 fans packed into the ground. Wrexham played well but not at their best, Liverpool were too worldly-wise to let them. A certain Kenny Dalglish was at his very best and helped himself to a hat trick as Liverpool emerged with a 3 - 1 win. In my most optimistic moments, I believe that we deserved a replay. But I can have no real argument with the final score. But who can forget that moment when Ray Clemence could only palm away Shinton's swerving snapshot and John Lyons raced in to ram the ball into the Kop net to make the score 1 - 1. In those sensational first half seconds, anything seemed possible but it just was not to be. In quarter-finals, for Wrexham, it just never seems to be.

The League Cup run was over. But there was still the FA Cup.

WREXHAM 1 v 0 BRISTOL CITY
Venue: The Racecourse
Attendance: 10,183

WREXHAM:
Dai Davies, Mickey Evans, Alan Dwyer, Gareth Davis, John Roberts, Mike Thomas, Bobby
Shinton, Mel Sutton, John Lyons, Graham Whittle, Les Cartwright
Manager: Arfon Griffiths
Scorer: Shinton

BRISTOL CITY:
John Shaw, Donnie Gillies, Gerry Sweeney, Gerry Gow, Gary Collier, Geoff Merrick, Trevor Tainton, Tom Ritchie, Keith Fear (John Bain), Jimmy Mann, Clive Whitehead
Manager: Alan Dicks

Referee: B. Martin

WREXHAM v BRISTOL CITY
FA CUP, 3RD ROUND REPLAY
Monday, 9 January, 1978

In the space of three seasons, between 1975 and 1978, Wrexham's average League attendances trebled from 4,000 to 12,000. I do not think that there is any better indicator of not just the success the club had enjoyed in the cups, but the style in which they had achieved it, a style that was on display week in, week out. And I can think of few better examples of this than the cup replay with Bristol City.

I have to say that generally the giant-killings which impress me the most are those which occur in replays. For, as we all know, the laws of TV punditry state that giant-killings occur when:

(a) the giant under-estimates the capabilities of the underdog;

(b) as a consequence of (a) above, the giant plays well below their capabilities;

(c) the underdog manages to play well above themselves on this one-off occasion;

(d) and as a result of (a), (b) and (c) above there is a giant-killing.

Replays are, by definition, not one-off occasions. If the giant has been dragged kicking and screaming to a replay, they are clearly no longer going into the unknown. They are aware of the under-dog's strengths and weaknesses. They know that they must play well to avoid a 'shock' and consequently should win.

Well, what of this third round tie then? This was to be the second and third time that the two sides had met this season: City had already lost to Wrexham in the League Cup. The draw for the third round of the FA Cup had presented the West Country outfit with the ideal opportunity, and a home tie at that, to gain sweet and swift revenge for their giant-killing.

Bristol City were continuing to find life very tough in the top-flight and were in 18th place in the table, just above the relegation zone. Wrexham were now sitting very proudly on top of the Third Division, having taken 33 points from 23 games. So Wrexham were now flying and City were struggling. But the fact remains that City were a First Division side and, something that should not be forgotten, would win their battle to remain a First Division giant. Going into this third round tie, I still had a vivid image of Tom Ritchie's *Match of the Day* goal, he was a good player and City were not a bad team.

'City are a side with a blend of stars and players who have been brought on by the club', Arfon Griffiths had said. The stars in the Bristol City galaxy included Scottish international Peter Cormack, a £100,000 signing from Liverpool, and a signing since the League Cup meeting, England international striker Joe Royle.

Wrexham, of course, had the fire-power of Dixie McNeil to call on in the FA Cup. Dixie had already scored in both of the earlier rounds when the mighty Reds had beaten non-league Burton Albion 2 - 0 at home and fellow promotion-chasers Preston North End at Deepdale by the same score.

As the third round tie at Ashton Gate got under way, City supporters must have felt comfortably sure that lightning would not strike twice as the red-shirted home side came out with all guns blazing and fired themselves into a two-goal lead inside the first 14 minutes.

But Wrexham, in their familiar white 'cup' shirts, were not about to lie down and, with 37 year old player manager Griffiths, playing his first competitive game in three months, in inspired form, they roared into life and took the First Division

Robins apart, scoring an amazing four goals in the process, with Dixie again on target. However, with the score at 2 - 4 and only five minutes of the game remaining, the drama was far from over as City then staged their own late, late fightback to earn a 4 - 4 draw thanks to goals from Cormack and, deep into the injury time, Kevin Mabbutt. But that goal, in earning City a replay, did not provide them with salvation, it was simply a stay of execution.

'I can't see a lot of goals again tonight', said Griffiths before the replay, 'because both camps are going to tighten up after conceding four'. He was to be half right.

Fifteen thousand fans packed into a noisy and excited the Racecourse. My dad and I arrived early as I wanted to secure the same spot in the Mold Road Paddock as we had occupied for the League Cup game. It was not that it offered the greatest view in the entire ground. It was just my little superstitious contribution to my team's cause. You may laugh, but who is to know what the final score-line would have been if that small area of concrete and red metal barrier had not been secured by me.

As the men in Wrexham red ran out to a mighty roar, there was only really one thought in my mind (not an unusual situation for me, I grant you!) — this was to be the night for another giant-killing. Defeat did not even seem a remote possibility. And almost from first kick to last, Wrexham turned on the most magical performance. It would be wrong to single out any one hero in a red shirt as they put on a flawless display. It was total attacking football all through the first half as the Third Division side dominated the midfield and ripped the City defence apart time and time again. The white-shirted First Division side clung on like a boxer on the ropes hoping for the saving sound of the bell. The mystery was that it took the awesome Robins almost half-an-hour to break the deadlock.

I had believed through all our games that Tom Ritchie would be a major influence. That night, he proved me to be a true pundit. But not, admittedly, in the way that I had perhaps envisaged and feared. As the ball trickled out towards us just inside the Wrexham half, Mr Ritchie trotted over, looking upfield to see who would be available from his throw-in. There was the white ball on the white touchline as Wrexham regrouped. He picked it up. The linesman immediately raised his flag and waved it with all the enthusiasm he could muster. The referee blew his whistle. It was handball — the ball had never crossed the line! Fifteen thousand people laughed. Ritchie could not believe his misfortune and, in frustration/temper/embarrassment, threw his toys out of the pram and drop-kicked the ball away into the Paddock. The referee booked him. Fifteen thousand people laughed even louder.

Laughter quickly turned to celebration. Left-back Alan Dwyer lofted the free-kick up towards the Tech end over the still-muttering Ritchie. Dixie McNeil coolly collected the ball and swept it, almost without looking, wide to Bobby Shinton on the left wing and sprinted away into the box. I stood on tip-toes to watch the Reds' N° 7 take the ball on before firing over a near-post cross which was met by Dixie who gave Shaw no chance with a header which flashed past him into the net. 1 - 0.

The floodgates were open. Five minutes later, City were stunned again as McNeil and Shinton repeated their combination. There was a superb drag-back by Shinton which wrong-footed the entire First Division defence, and most of the away fans behind the Tech End goal, and he slid the ball across to Graham Whittle in space on the edge of the 18-yard box. BANG! 2 - 0.

City were completely demoralised and, having no effective creative response to Wrexham's quality, began to kick out at anything moving forward in a red shirt in the vicinity of a ball. The rugged Gow was booked for a foul on Dwyer. Collier then tried to collect Shinton's legs as a souvenir of the occasion and became their third yellow card statistic. And Wrexham still continued to surge forward maintaining their siege on the City goal. With the half-time whistle imminent, Mickey Thomas collected the ball on the edge of the penalty area. As the massed defence advanced towards him, Thomas went one way, then the other. He looked up and, seeing Shaw inches off his line, delivered the most immaculate left foot chip. The crowd knew the ball's destiny and the celebrations began even before it flew over Shaw's failing hands into the net. 3 - 0.

I had never heard such a crescendo of appreciative noise for a team leaving the field at half-time. It had been 45 minutes of the most breath-taking brilliance. For a Third Division side to be leading a team from the premier League by such a margin was unbelievable. But, in truth, the gulf between the two teams in that half was far wider than the three goals. Eager as I was for the second half to commence, I did not think that the game was over. City had already managed a two-goal Houdini act on Saturday and I knew that they would have to come out and go for broke. I thought that Wrexham might try to, understandably, sit back and look to hit the over-committed white shirts on the break.

But, to my amazement, it was Wrexham who again took the initiative immediately, with Griffiths and Sutton making the centre of midfield their own. Ten minutes in and the score should have been extended to 4 - 0 as Shinton jinked his way into the box before being brought down by Merrick. The Kop were already celebrating the next goal as Shinton picked himself up and placed the ball on the spot in front of them. Wrexham's attacking maestro stepped up and hit his shot low. I got ready to leap at the familiar sight of the ball exploding into the net, but Shaw dived to brilliantly beat the ball away. At 3 - 0 up, the crowd could afford to feel generous and we clapped the keeper's efforts.

The second half was not the same pounding performance from Wrexham. They controlled the game. They knew that City were a devastated and demoralised team. McNeil was withdrawn from the fray to a tremendous ovation and on came John

Lyons who was soon characteristically in the middle of the action as he burst through the shell shocked remnants of the visitors' defence, only to be floored by Collier's foul. Penalty number two!

Up stepped Shinton again. From the Paddock, I could see that Shaw was engaged in a spot of 'sporting' banter with the Reds' ace. This time, the Kop were not taking things for granted. Shinton breezed in again. Shaw dived to his left. The ball went to his right. But our cheers were premature as the ball cannoned against the inside of the post and flashed across the goalline to the waiting goalkeeper. Shinton just stood there in disbelief.

'One Bobby Shinton', the Kop began singing, 'there's only one Bobby Shinton' and on they went. The showman looked up and applauded his audience's support. At the final whistle, City had only managed to force Dai Davies into one real save from Gow's strike in the closing minutes and the carnival had started long before the final whistle. Wrexham's victory was more comprehensive and convincing than even the 3 - 0 scoreline suggested. It could, without any imagination whatsoever, have been 5 - 0 if those two penalties had been converted.

Wrexham's three goal scorers against Bristol City: Mickey Thomas,
Dixie McNeil and Graham Whittle. [Wrexham Leader]

I can always remember that, after the Reds had slaughtered promotion candidates Tranmere Rovers 6 - 1 at the Racecourse later in the season, the loudspeakers played *Oh, Oh, Oh, it's Magic* as we left the ground. I do not remember what song was playing as we made our exit after the Bristol game, but it should have been that one because after all, *Another One Bites the Dust* had yet to be written!

'We played out of our skins tonight', said a proud Arfon Griffiths after the match. 'I have seen goals equal to the ones we got, but never in the same match'. Another admirer of Wrexham's polished performance that night was Liverpool manager Bob Paisley who was full of praise for the 'magnificent' Reds. A disconsolate City manager, Alan Dicks, pondered the completeness of his side's humiliation and observed 'the last time we were so bad was when we played Wrexham in the League Cup!' He added graciously that 'Wrexham are a credit to the Third Division, they proved that on Saturday and again tonight. They showed us how to play and will give anyone a hard match on this ground'.

As Mr Dicks and his First Division side left the Racecourse that night, they must surely have drawn some comfort from the fact that there was no possibility of them having to face Wrexham again this season! And Wrexham moved on from First Division Robins to First Division Magpies.

WREXHAM 3 v 0 BRISTOL CITY
Venue: The Racecourse
Attendance: 15,614

WREXHAM:
Dai Davies, Alan Hill, Alan Dwyer, Gareth Davis, Wayne Ciegelski, Mike Thomas, Bobby Shinton, Mel Sutton, Dixie McNeil (John Lyons), Graham Whittle, Arfon Griffiths
Manager: Arfon Griffiths
Scorers: McNeil, Whittle, Thomas

BRISTOL CITY:
John Shaw, Gerry Sweeney, Donnie Gillies, Gerry Gow, Gary Collier, Geoff Merrick, Trevor Tainton, Tom Ritchie, Joe Royle, Kevin Mabbutt, Peter Cormack
Manager: Alan Dicks

Referee: R. Perkin

WREXHAM v NEWCASTLE UNITED
FA CUP, 4TH ROUND REPLAY
Monday, 6 February, 1978

Of course, the name of Newcastle United is synonymous with giant-killing exploits. Unfortunately, if you're a fan of the black and white stripes, it's for all the wrong reasons. Every year at third round time, television dusts off that classic clip of non-league Hereford United's Ronnie Radford negotiating his way through the Edgar Street Somme-like mud, a one-two, and that sensational 25-yard pile-driver flies into the Newcastle net past Willie McFaul's classic goalkeeping dive. Only Newcastle fans tend to remember that, the week after the Hereford game, the Geordies went to Old Trafford and won.

When a little club gets drawn against Newcastle, memories of Ronnie Radford are never far away. After the demolition of Bristol City in the previous round, Reds' fans needed little encouragement to believe that their team could go to St. James' Park and win this fourth round tie.

Newcastle were, are ,a giant of a club in every sense. They had been the FA Cup finalists in 1974 and had finished fifth from top of the First Division in 1977. In the north-east, there had been the greatest of expectations going into this season, but these high aspirations had been undermined by both a players' revolt over contracts and a long list of injuries. Instead of being the anticipated title contenders, the Magpies had dropped into the relegation zone as early as September and had not managed to claw their way out of the bottom three ever since. The FA Cup was Newcastle's lifeline on a season of serious under-achievement. Standing in their way were the giant-killers, Wrexham FC.

The Geordies certainly had the players to go a long way in the Cup. Former Manchester United striker Alan Gowling had been the First Division top scorer in 1976 and he was well-supported by Northern Ireland international Tommy Cassidy, Micky Burns (a £170,000 signing from Blackpool) and Mark McGee (a £100,000 transfer from Scottish side Morton). Wrexham now lay in fourth place in Division Three, one point behind leaders Tranmere, and because of their successful runs in the League and FA Cups, had an incredible five games in hand on the front-runners.

'Welcome Wrexham', the programme notes for the game at St James' Park read. 'We say that guardedly, not at all sure if the Welsh side is going to provide entry to the fifth round. Rarely can the credentials of a side from two divisions lower have been looked at with such respect. But that should be the full extent. Wrexham are not Bastia, Forest or Liverpool. In any case the side which mainly concerns Bill McGarry is his own. When that is right, Wrexham's are there for the taking ...' The game at Newcastle was a tense affair played out in front of 28,000 fans and the *Match of the Day* cameras. My team seemingly becoming a regular part of my Saturday night treat, that was impressive.

Goalless at half-time on a dreadful mudbath pitch, Wrexham had not been able to find anything like the kind of form they had found in the previous round. Newcastle then took the lead from a right-wing corner with Bird climbing high to loop a header over the stranded Dai Davies into the net. But the Reds hit back almost instantly. From Thomas's left-wing cross, Dixie McNeil ran on to power in a header which Mahoney could only parry along the line. Before any defender could react to the threat, the ball was tucked into the goal by Dixie as he followed his first effort in.

But Newcastle again took the lead as Blackhall rampaged down the right touchline and, as everyone waited for his centre, including Dai Davies, he blasted the ball into the net at the near post from a ridiculously tight angle. The home crowd went wild. Dai looked suitably under whelmed.

The final score was to be 2 - 2 which was, on balance, a fair reflection of the game. However, it had looked like the Reds would be going home without their just desserts until Dixie grabbed his second goal moments from the end. And what a sensational goal it was. Again a cross from the left instigated the danger. This time, the provider was full-back Dwyer. The alert Shinton glanced the ball on; his deflection sending the ball over the Newcastle defenders to the far side of the box to where, no coincidence at all, Dixie was just arriving. Without breaking his stride, Dixie lashed an effortless left-foot half volley into the net. It is a sign of true greatness to make something so difficult look so easy. Mahoney never saw the ball. It was the perfect strike. St. James' Park was stunned. Dixie raised both arms aloft and looked up thankfully into the murky north-east sky. It was, without doubt, a goal made in heaven.

'I don't think that we were at our best, but we showed a lot of courage and character to come from behind twice against a First Division side', said Arfon after the game. 'Newcastle United is never an easy place to get a result'.

As he looked forward to the replay on Welsh soil, Arfon cautioned, 'I don't go along with those people who have made us favourites to win the replay. It's another game, we both start fresh and Newcastle will know more about our ability and capabilities'. Arfon, though, was very much in the minority as most Reds' fans, myself included, expected nothing less than victory that night, knowing as we did our team's ability and capabilities. Added spice was given to the replay by the draw for the fifth round. The winners of this tie would have a home game against north-east non-leaguers, Blyth Spartans. The incentive was clear for both sides: Only the non-leaguers would stand between them and the FA Cup quarter-finals. And the Tynesiders, in particular, must have fancied the prospect of a nice little local derby to get there.

In fact, the mighty Reds needed just 80 seconds to get their, by now, well-rehearsed giant-killing show well and truly on the road to the next round. In their first attack, kicking into the Kop end, Shinton swept the ball into the Newcastle area. Dixie and his marker, John Bird, both jumped for the ball. In the challenge, the ball ballooned up into the air once more towards the left-hand corner of the six-yard box. The first to react was, of course, Dixie and as the ball dropped, he swivelled to hook the most fantastic left-foot volley on the turn into the back of the net. 1 - 0.

What a start! It was natural to expect the First Division outfit to be stung into life by this early setback. But the truth is that for the next half-hour, Wrexham played them off the park. Wrexham were so dominant and superior that it was almost embarrassing. The prime tormentor was the bandy-legged bearded magician, Bobby Shinton, who conjured up every trick that he had ever learnt. But he was not alone. Les Cartwright and Mickey Thomas were in command down the left wing, Mel Sutton was his usual solid self, while Whittle and Dixie caused complete havoc down the middle. Newcastle were over-run, but chance after chance went begging. With five minutes to go until half-time, it was a mystery that would have perplexed Mulder and Scully as to how Wrexham had failed to increase their lead, if not made the game completely safe.

Then our comfortable world turned upside down. Newcastle's highly rated Under-23 international Irving Nattrass discovered Wrexham's penalty area cunningly hidden at the other end of the field. Micky Burns raced into the previously unexplored territory of Wrexham's box to meet Nattrass' cross with his head. There was a deflection off John Roberts and, the next thing we knew, Dai Davies was retrieving the ball from the net. 1 - 1.

Newcastle players and supporters clearly could not believe their good fortune. The stunned Kop chanted its defiance. For Wrexham, this could have been a sickening blow from which mere ordinary teams fall to pieces. But Wrexham hit back instantly.

Newcastle seemed content with their slice of luck and sat back in defence looking to hold tightly onto what they had got until half-time. The psychological advantage would undoubtedly have been theirs if they were to emerge from the tunnel for the second half on level terms.

One moment of sheer Shinton genius shattered their plans. The Reds' number seven collected the ball in his usual casual manner wide on the right of midfield. Almost every player in a black and white shirt was behind the ball marking a red shirt. Shinton moved forward and in-field beating one man, then another until he faced a wall of Newcastle defenders on the edge of the penalty area. As he looked up to power in a shot, Mahoney advanced a couple of yards to narrow the angle. With brilliant awareness and true skill, Shinton picked his spot and launched the most delicate chip over the back-scrambling 'keeper, under the crossbar and into the net. 2 - 1.

Shinton, the showman, celebrated in style as the home crowd worshipped their idol. The Kop never sang truer words; there really was only one Bobby Shinton. Newcastle came out after the break and certainly put in the effort to try to avert the inevitable giant-killing. Roberts and Davis confidently kept things under control in defence and, in midfield, Thomas, Sutton and Whittle were as effective at preventing the opposition from settling on the ball as they were at kick-starting every Wrexham move.

The Robins never made the mistake of trying to sit too far back and simply cling on to their precious one-goal lead. Wrexham never really looked in danger and we should have had a penalty when Whittle's drive was blocked by Bird's outstretched hand. With seven minutes left, a mistake by Blackhall allowed Whittle a clear run at goal. Mahoney raced out to intercept, but Whittle nonchalantly and unselfishly slid the ball across to the unmarked Dixie and Wrexham's number nine did not make mistakes from six yards with an open goal in front of him. 3 - 1.

The crowd knew that the cup-tie was now over. The Magpies, too, seemed to recognise the inevitable. But they continued to press forward, their magnificent travelling fans deserved that much. With the seconds drifting away, a long ball out of the Newcastle defence found Gowling in space just inside the Wrexham half. The striped shirts surged vainly forward. Without looking, Gowling knocked the ball back out towards the right-back position. Unfortunately for him, and his team, the Newcastle right-back was hurtling further ahead down the right-wing. Even more unfortunately for him and his now braking colleagues, Wrexham's left-winger Les Cartwright was the recipient of the ball and, with a wide open space in front of him, he sped towards goal unchallenged. Mahoney moved out to greet him and again had the indignity, but by now familiar sight, of watching the ball lobbed over his head from the edge of the box. 4 - 1.

It was a classy finish which summed up yet another memorable, outstanding performance. Wrexham had won convincingly, but not easily. It is the mark of a class side and quality players to make the difficult look simple and the virtually impossible look ridiculously possible. Arfon Griffiths looked back on the game with great satisfaction. 'We played as we normally do against First Division sides … Some people have said that Newcastle are a bad side. They might have been on the night, but I like to think that they did not play well because we did not let them'.

I remember eating my breakfast the next morning; the *Daily Express* laid carefully alongside my plate of toast. 'WREXHAM WRECKS 'EM' the back page proclaimed. It was a great headline. I was ready for school.

The fifth round draw now, of course, gave the north-east a chance for swift revenge and also turned the tables on Wrexham as the Reds became the red-hot favourites against non-league 'giant-killers' Blyth, who had already conquered Stoke City.

There was a crowd of almost 20,000 to watch the Third Division leaders take on the amateurs. The Racecourse pitch was bone-hard with many players on both sides opting to wear trainers for the game. Blyth played with fierce passion and commitment and deservedly took the lead when Reds' full-back Alan Hill seemingly mistook the Spartans for a registered charity and gave generously with a badly under-hit back pass to Dai Davies. Blyth striker Terry Johnson appreciated the donation and sent a few thousand Geordies at the Tech end into Geordie heaven with the opening goal. And a shock looked on the cards for the rest of the wintry afternoon. For all Wrexham's skill and creativity, a combination of the green and white shirts and unforgiving pitch prevented the Wrexham cup machine from warming up. I suppose, looking back, the pitch was pretty lethal and the game should not have been played. But the referee gave the go-ahead and you have to give a lot of credit to the non-leaguers who were prepared to risk almost anything to get a result; this match, after all, represented their entire season and for some, their whole footballing careers. For Wrexham, it would be too simplistic to say that this was just another game as the league title and promotion were the horizon on which the club's eyes were focused.

But that was probably a major influence on the day. As the minutes drained away, we knew that it was all over and tonight we would have to suffer Wrexham, our famous giant-killers, being 'giant-killed' on *Match of the Day*. I thought I might forego my Saturday treat on this one-off occasion. As the 90 minute mark approached, a steady stream of dejected red and white-scarved fans began to drift away. 'Come on', my dad said quietly and we began to pick our way slowly out of the crowded Mold Road Paddock. I was now having to contemplate unthinkable defeat. Then, suddenly, there were a few hopeful shouts and we turned to see Bobby Shinton working his way down the left wing towards the Tech end. A tackle went in and the ball rolled out of play. CORNER! The Kop roared. This had to be the last chance. We strained to see down the far end of the ground. Cartwright trotted over, he fiddled with the corner flag and then sent over a near-post cross. Under pressure, the goalkeeper fisted the ball away for another corner. The hopeful Kop roared even louder. Cartwright again toyed with the corner flag. Then over came the centre. But the goalkeeper was there and made an easy catch. Now it was the turn of the Blyth fans to roar, but theirs had the sound of victory.

For the first time that afternoon, I realised how cold it was. We turned to leave. But, no, the game was still alive. The referee had ordered the corner to be retaken. I did not know why until *Match of the Day* that night. Apparently the corner flag was not in the frozen ground when the corner kick had been taken. Cartwright struggled to get the flag upright. Eventually, he was ready and fired in a vicious in-swinging corner. The goalkeeper was struggling as the ball curled over him towards the far post as big John Roberts stormed in, following in his wake was Dixie McNeil and — if I close my eyes I can still see that moment perfectly — the distant crowd of players at the back-post and then the white net billowing. I could not quite believe it. I remember looking instantly for the man in black and felt a warm glow sweep through my body as I saw him running back pointing to the centre spot. It was a GOAL! We had equalised! I looked around me to double-check my joy:

Incredible noise. Incredible elation. Incredible relief. And who else but Dixie McNeil could have poached such a vital goal. 1 - 1.

The decibels hit a level where I was beyond being able to hear the sound. The people, the noise, the stadium were one and the Kop sang on and on. It was not until *Match of the Day* that night that I knew the full extent of our good luck. Yes, there was the pantomime of the corner flag. But the camera clearly showed that the last-minute corner won by Bobby Shinton should, no doubt about it, have been a goal-kick as the ball ricocheted off the Reds' striker's distinctive white trainers. After the game, the referee even acknowledged his error in awarding that corner.

For the replay, the entire north-east were fired up to see the non-leaguers get their justice. The game was played at Newcastle's St. James' Park and a staggering 40,000 plus fans packed in. The frost of the previous weeks had now thawed into a bottomless puddle of water and mud. Though Blyth battled hard, Wrexham's quality and composure was there for all to see. Graham Whittle lashed in the hardest-hit penalty I have ever seen and Dixie scored probably the goal of the season, a sliding first time left-foot half volley from the edge of the penalty area which flew across and past the Blyth 'keeper into the top corner. A 2 - 0 lead and Dai Davies played the entire second half with a damaged hand. Blyth, yelled on by the partisan crowd, put the Reds under a tremendous amount of pressure and deserved the goal they scored. But it was Wrexham's cup dream that lived on.

The quarter-final was played on 11 March and brought First Division Arsenal to the Racecourse. Every player of theirs was a household name: Pat Jennings; Pat Rice; Sammy Nelson; David Price; David O'Leary; Willie Young; Liam Brady; Alan Sunderland; Malcolm MacDonald; Graham Rix; Alan Hudson.

I still have the *Evening Leader's* souvenir supplement issued before the big game. It contains a reader's letter articulating, with the kind of self-confidence that even Ron Atkinson can only dream about, that 1978 would see a Wrexham v Nottingham Forest final. Even back then when I read it, I thought the logic was decidedly dodgy. But, on the eve of such a match, you like to hope that maybe ...

But, as it turned out, if the fate of the cup was written in the stars, the

Dixie McNeil.

handwriting must have been absolutely appalling. The final was to be
an Arsenal v Ipswich event.

Arsenal coach Don Howe,
however, was certainly wary of the
'Ides of March' as his all-stars
prepared for the game. Wrexham
had done little to soothe any London
nerves by warming up for the sixth
round with a midweek 6 - 1 demolition of fellow promotion-chasers
Tranmere at the Racecourse. Howe,
a highly respected figure in the
game, had witnessed this massacre
and had nothing but total respect for
the Third Division team. 'We know
we must find our best form to win
this one', he said. 'They beat Bristol and Newcastle and, although I admit those two
are not top of Division One, they are not bad sides. We shall play this match as
though we're facing a team that is top of the First Division'.

Arsenal won the game 3 - 2. The First Division side did not deserve to win. The
Third Division side certainly did not deserve to lose. Referees have a difficult job to
do and are, I'm led to believe, human. And so, if we accept that premise, they are
bound to make mistakes. We all make mistakes, that is why Mr Tippex is a very
wealthy man. If referees did not get things wrong, of course, our dream would
probably have ended at home to Blyth. After the 'saving' corner against the
Spartans, it would be wrong to bemoan our luck, or lack of it, against Arsenal. I am
sure that there are people up there in the north-east today who still feel 'cheated',
who still believe that their brave non-league warriors had earned their place in the
quarter-final (which could have been their ever-lasting moment of glory), who
would still like to take that fickle finger of fate and feed it to a passing piranha.

But, that accepted, it is worth recording that the corner from which Arsenal
scored the crucial second goal should have been a goal-kick as the ball rebounded
off Liam Brady's boot, not Alan Dwyer's. And, for the life of me, I cannot
understand the reason why referee Tom Reynolds disallowed what should have been
the opening goal of the game for Wrexham when Bobby Shinton hooked the ball
into the net. For his all-round handling of the game, it would be an under-statement
to say, Mr Reynolds did not endear himself to the home crowd.

The game was not just about the referee though. Eddie Niedzwiecki, in goal for the injured Dai, was not at his best. Perhaps, I wondered afterwards, had those penalties of mine caused lasting doubts or was it the early 'roughing up' by Malcolm MacDonald that had caused Eddie's uncharacteristic tentativeness? But, overall, Wrexham played well and if Les Cartwright had tucked away that late chance … Know me, know my 'we were robbed but I'd rather play well and lose than bore them to defeat' speech. What else can you do except celebrate the quality of your team's performance?

I think what hurt the most was not the defeat, or even the dubious decisions. It was, for me anyway, the fact that we had had the 'rub' against Blyth. We had been dead and buried and then salvation. You really begin to wonder if there is a date with destiny looming. Why give us that last minute Lazarus moment, only for 'lucky' Arsenal to destroy these newly constructed fortified hopes?

As the final whistle sounded on the Reds' cup run, the entire Wrexham team looked totally dejected. So the dream was over again in the quarter-finals. But neither on the pitch or off it, Wrexham were not to go quietly into the night. 'WREXHAM! WREXHAM! WREXHAM!' the home crowd roared proudly and defiantly. And the crescendo of noise was not just coming from the Kop — the Yale stand, the Yale Paddock, the Plas Coch stand, the Mold Road Paddock, everyone wanted to salute their heroes. No-one wanted to leave. This moment will always live with me as the defining moment of the unity, the feeling of togetherness and the sheer spine-tingling red-blooded pride that the cup engenders in Wrexham fans and players.

Arsenal's own 'Super Mac', Malcolm MacDonald, saluted the Reds' performance after the game. 'Wrexham are the best team we have played all season', he said. 'And I'm not just talking about cup games. They caused us more problems than any other team has done and that includes Liverpool and Nottingham Forest. I cannot give them a better testimony than that and my opinion is shared by all the lads in our dressing room. As for promotion, Wrexham will walk it'.

In the cup, Arsenal cruised past Second Division Orient in the semi-final to face Ipswich at Wembley as the hottest of favourites. 'Osborne, 1 - 0!' screamed David Coleman. Arsenal lost.

You cannot help but think of what could have been. Wrexham had already beaten two First Division sides that season alone and so, if decisions had gone our way and we had defeated Arsenal (go with me on this), it clearly does not demand too great a leap of faith to believe that Wrexham could have beaten Orient in the semi. I back that up with further 'evidence', we played Orient twice the following season and beat them 1 - 0 away and 3 - 1 at home. It could so easily have been Wrexham at Wembley lining up against Ipswich. We certainly would not have been outclassed, would we? Paradise lost!

While in the other quarter-final seasons (past and future) the momentum of a cup run undermined the League campaign, this was the year that everything went absolutely perfectly. The cup disappointment only seemed to increase the players' desire and games-in-hand were quickly converted into points in the bag.

Forget the promotion near-miss of 1974. Forget the abject misery of last season — wipe away that Crystal Palace game and the memory of Mansfield (they were actually being relegated back down). This time our team delivered. Rotherham United arrived on 22 April 1978 and half an hour into the game were 5 - 0 down. At the end, Wrexham were 7 - 1 winners. Graham Whittle had helped himself to a hat-trick. The club had helped themselves to promotion. Now that's doing it in style.

On 7 October 1977, the rock band Queen released *We are the Champion*s. I had always recognised the many and self-evident talents of Messrs. Mercury, May, Taylor and Deacon but it was at this point that I felt the need to add telepathy to the list. It was also meant to be as the Third Division championship was wrapped up.

I remember Burnley Chairman Bob Lord presenting the trophy to Gareth Davis before the final home league game. The team then went on a euphoric lap of honour in front of some 20,000 fans. The Robins had finally landed in the Second Division for the first time ever, after 57 years in the League's lower divisions.

The final game was a dull 0-0 draw. No-one cared. We had enjoyed the most mesmerising entertainment all season, virtually every visiting team had been taken apart. Tremendous times. On Sundays I would be waiting impatiently for the next Saturday.

Could it really have been over twenty years ago? I can still, without hesitation, name the team. Could there ever be another season like that one?

Fans have often debated whose team it was that won promotion — John Neal's or Arfon Griffiths'. The answer for me is simple. It was theirs — and ours. It was like a great movie. All the elements were right to entertain and excite. A great script which engaged every emotion and which had the ideal ending, solid direction, talented stars, a reliable supporting cast, a brilliant setting and, we, the crowd, the ultimate soundtrack, able to complement the action and, when there was the occasional lull, fill the void with meaningful, heart-felt noise. Together, something wonderful in the history of Wrexham FC was created. Like all great films, you want to live through it over and over again.

Champions of the Third Division and, let us not forget, winners of the Welsh Cup — Wrexham had defeated Second Division Cardiff City 2 - 0 at Ninian Park in the semi-final and Bangor City were beaten in the two-legged final. An open-top bus ride around the town with thousands lining the streets to hail their heroes. Our very own double season.

But even those two triumphs do not really begin to tell the story. Quarter-finalists in the FA Cup. Quarter-finalists in the League Cup. A place in the European Cup

Winners' Cup secured. The magazine *Reveille* voted Wrexham the first ever winners of their 'Giant-Killers Cup'. A season to remember. Forever.

The legendary Bill Shankly, who watched Wrexham many times that season and was no mean judge of a decent football team, described the 1977–78 Wrexham side as 'the best team ever promoted from the Third Division to the Second'. You cannot argue with that. Thanks for the memories guys.

WREXHAM 4 v 1 NEWCASTLE UNITED
Venue: The Racecourse
Attendance: 18,676

WREXHAM:
Dai Davies, Alan Hill, Alan Dwyer, Gareth Davis, John Roberts, Mike Thomas, Bobby Shinton, Mel Sutton, Dixie McNeil, Graham Whittle, Les Cartwright
Manager: Arfon Griffiths
Scorers: McNeil (2), Shinton, Cartwright

NEWCASTLE:
Mike Mahoney, Ray Blackhall, Mick Barker, Irving Nattrass, John Bird, John Blackley (Tommy Cassidy), Stewart Barraclough, Micky Burns, Mark McGee, Alan Gowling, Alan Kennedy
Manger: Bill McGarry
Scorer: Roberts (OG)

Referee: C. Seel

NOTTINGHAM FOREST v WREXHAM
FA CUP, 3RD ROUND
Saturday, 2 January, 1982

The 1977–78 season was undoubtedly the greatest year ever for Wrexham FC. All through the school summer holidays I was waiting, hungry for the new season to start. I had never wished away those July and August weeks before; a new school term had always been an effective deterrent there. But such was the power of that football team that I never doubted, never questioned for one second that there would be anything other than a continuation of where the team had left off. I suppose that I should have realised that things just do not, cannot, get any better than that. But the pessimist in me was still lacking maturity.

I had only optimism for the new season. After all, we had taken on eight First Division giants over the previous two seasons and, of the twelve games which we had played in total against them, Wrexham had only lost three. It was a record which certainly impressed me. The Second Division could hold no fears for my team.

Up to this point, my entire Wrexham League career had been focused on the elusive grail, promotion. I do not think that I had ever really acknowledged that there were two ends to a Division, a bottom as well as a top. The club's four seasons in the Second Division were to complete my education on this as I understood for the first time that when you're standing in the middle of a ladder, there are two very different directions in which you can go ... and gravity was not on our side.

So, well, maybe a Second Division side defeating a First Division side should not truly be classed a 'giant-killing'. But, sadly, this was a Wrexham side who were going to plunge into the Third Division at the end of the season playing away at the 1979 and 1980 European Champions.

As the Robins went into the game, the writing was already daubed on the relegation wall. It had been another season plagued by injuries and inconsistent performances. The omens had not been good before it had even begun with manager Arfon Griffiths resigning when told to cut back on his staff to save cash. It was a sad end to Griffiths' long service with the club. He was the back-bone of the club's success through the 'Seventies, scoring a total of 120 goals from midfield. To many Reds' supporters he is *the* Wrexham player of all time; the complete embodiment of everything that the club stands for, hard-working, honest and stylish, forever ready to attack and play the game the way that its inventors would always have wished it to be played.

Arfon was replaced by his assistant Mel Sutton. But the new manager brought no new luck to the Reds' Second Division odyssey. Now, in January, Wrexham were sitting uncomfortably in 20th place, third from bottom, having taken only 18 points. Forest were in seventh place in Division One and their manager, the quietly spoken, shy and retiring Brian Clough had already experienced too many disappointments in the FA Cup (a trophy which he never won) to take anything for granted. Speaking before the game, he warned, 'I shouldn't have to remind anyone about the potential Wrexham have for giant-killing in cup competitions. In fact, it's not merely potential we are talking about because our opponents have actually gone out and conquered over the years. Their track record as a cup side is well-known and any side that has under-estimated them in the past has done so at very considerable cost'. High praise indeed from another of football's legends.

Reds' striker Mick Vinter, a £150,000 signing from Notts County in June 1979,

Mick Vinter.

had once been on schoolboy forms with Forest and sounded a warning to the giants before the game. 'Wrexham have upset more than their fair share in recent years', he said. 'The club have a strong cup tradition and, although on paper we have little chance against Forest, in many ways that's an enviable position to be in. It means we have nothing to lose and can enjoy ourselves, and from what I've seen of Forest on television, they are not the side they were'.

Of course, it was also true that Wrexham were not the side they were. Many of the class of 1978 had gone. Individually, there was still considerable talent all through the Wrexham side but somehow they were rarely able to function as a team. But they had managed to show tantalising glimpses of former glories earlier in the season. In the League Cup, the Reds pulled off a highly impressive 2 - 0 victory away at Luton Town, the runaway leaders of the Second Division.

There was no doubt that this Wrexham side, on their day, could match any team. It did seem, though, that this season, their day was never a Saturday! But this third round FA Cup tie was to be played at the City Ground on New Year's Day, a Friday. There was hope … but dense fog in Nottingham forced the game to be put back 24 hours to … Saturday. What followed was a classic game of two halves.

Forest started strongly and forced Wrexham, again in their white shirts, to defend. After barely two minutes, the First Division side won a free-kick 25 yards out from the Wrexham goal. Eddie Niedzwiecki, now Wrexham's number one and clearly completely rehabilitated from that infant penalty shoot-out trauma, organised his wall as Mark Proctor waited. Proctor then raced up and hit a rasping drive into the wall. The ball struck Dixie McNeil's left boot and the vicious deflection sent the ball sailing past the helpless Wrexham 'keeper and into the net. 1 - 0 to Forest.

An unlucky goal down, dejected faces, a bitterly cold day, 88 long, marathon minutes to go. The footballing gods were clearly not feeling particularly Welsh. At that moment, one or two New Year resolutions were severely tested. While the City Ground partied, Wrexham fans had the look of an archbishop at an Iron Maiden concert. The whole season seemed to be summed up in those luckless, miserable seconds. Wrexham just could not get their game together as Forest dominated the midfield and pressed for a second goal. Red-haired Ian Wallace was a constant threat with both Ciegelski and former Colchester centre-half Steve Dowman struggling to keep him at bay. Hero of the first half, though, was Niedzwiecki who made two crucial saves. In fact, Eddie was one of the few success stories of this sorry season.

At half-time, the Robins were still only 1 - 0 down. Manager Mel Sutton was convinced that the tie was still alive. 'You can still win', he told his players. He then set out the strategy for the second half, 'keep battling and feed Steve Fox'.

When Steve Fox was hungry for the ball, there was not a defence in the country, or Europe, which could stifle his appetite for tearing teams apart. Foxie was a £90,000 buy from Birmingham City in December 1978 and had a reputation for being something of a rebel off the pitch. He was not the club's most consistent performer. He was, however, at his best, as exciting, as fast and as skilful as any player I have ever seen wearing a Wrexham shirt, a turbo-charged Bobby Shinton. The fans loved him and voted him their player of the year last season. There was no arguing that he had the talent to become an England international, he once tore promotion chasing Sheffield Wednesday apart single-handedly.

The second half saw Fox at his very best. Wrexham came out in fighting mood, determined to give it a go. Fox immediately made his intentions plain when he forced Peter Shilton to dive low to block his right-foot drive. and, soon after, had the England goalkeeper gratefully watching as another long range effort shaved the crossbar. Wrexham were on top and Forest were on the rack. But, as Terry Venables once rightly informed ITV viewers, you have to score goals to win matches.

From a corner, the battling Billy Ronson found the rampant Fox. The winger looked up and picked out Dowman with a precise, delicate cross which the dark-haired defender powered into the net. 1 - 1.

Wrexham maintained their stranglehold of the game from the restart, giving Forest no time to settle and rebuild their composure. Nine minutes on and, incredibly, Wrexham took the lead. Ronson, Wrexham's new midfield dynamo who seemed to get more bookings than the local travel agents, stood over a free-kick, some 25 yards from goal. He rolled the ball to Vinter who cracked an unstoppable shot into the top corner, with Shilton grabbing air. 2 - 1!

Wrexham's magical 12 minute spell was completed when Fox again weaved his way down the right before firing in another dangerous cross; this one was met on the volley by the deadly boot of Dixie McNeil and Shilton knew exactly where to find the ball. 3 - 1!

For three sides of the City Ground, their New Year party had been well and truly gate-crashed. The Forest players looked bemused at the scoreline. The Wrexham team, too, looked bemused at the scoreline. The only difference being that that the white shirts looked bemused with huge smiles. And the Wrexham fans sang away in disbelieving delight. Happy New Year!

There was some expected late pressure as the First Division side sought to save the day and themselves from a roasting from their manager. But Eddie stood tall and then the unexpected celebrations began. The result was proclaimed nationally as the giant-killing of the round. It was a brilliant victory; the highlight of the season. It was also to be the high point of Mel Sutton's brief managerial career.

The next round saw the Reds drawn away at fellow Division Two side, Chelsea. The manager of the blues was one John Neal, a man who knew more than most about the giant killing reputation of the Welsh club. In the build-up to the game, he hailed his former club's 'remarkable 3 - 1 triumph at Nottingham Forest', but added, 'I can't remember many occasions when I wanted the Robins to lose'. It was a difficult tie. But then you think if we can beat Forest away …

Wrexham did not lose at Stamford Bridge. They did not win either. The game was a tense and tight goalless draw. A very respectable result, a replay at the Racecourse. Mission accomplished. The replay also produced a 0-0 stalemate.

Wrexham won the toss for home advantage in the second replay. For the first 80 minutes, there was only one side in it. Unfortunately, they wore blue shirts and scored two goals. The hobbling Vinter nicked a goal for Wrexham just before the end which led to a late flurry in the Chelsea penalty area and, at last and at least, gave us something to shout about. We shouted and hoped against hope that someone in a red shirt would find a moment, a golden second of inspiration. But deep down I knew that it was not going to happen.

The season now held nothing but a fight for Division Two survival. Throughout the 'Seventies, I had gone along to watch the Reds expecting them to win every game. In fact, it was much more than that, I believed totally that we would win every game. In fact, again, it was much, much more than that. I believed unequivocally that we would thrash any team who dared to line up against us. In the promotion year, it was a profound shock when an opposing team had the audacity to even score against my team. It seemed to me completely contrary to the laws of nature. My team were too good to concede goals; it could not happen. Whenever they did score, I can always remember looking immediately for the referee, convinced that he would disallow it. You can imagine the trauma that defeat could cause. That season, there was not much trauma. Happy days. Brilliant days.

The Racecourse was indeed our fortress and we walked up the Mold Road with as much confidence as any home supporter entering Anfield, Old Trafford or anywhere. Those days were gone. The 1981–82 season ended with Wrexham second from bottom of the Second Division. 44 points, 11 wins, 11 draws, 22 defeats. Relegated. I had come to the stark realisation that my team were very much mortal two years back. Belief in victory had been replaced by simply a hope of victory.

Joey Jones.

This, in turn, had been substituted by just the hope of avoiding defeat. I was now disorientated. I had even gone through a stage of wondering if I was some kind of jinx on the team and, perhaps, if I did not turn up, my team would win. But what if I did not attend and they did win, would I then have to stay away as long as they continued to win? Or what if I did not turn up and they won but the jinx had been someone else who had not turned up so that I could have attended after all and seen the win and ... However, while I had clearly lost my faith, I never thought that we would be relegated

Relegation did not stab at my emotions like the devastating promotion miss in 1977. It did not seem real. Of course I knew that it was, there seemed to be Shrewsbury supporters appearing from everywhere to make sure that this event had not passed me by (Shrewsbury remained in the Second Division). I knew we were down, but just because it was true, that did not mean that I had to accept it. I mean, look at the team. This was a reasonable set of players. Not world beaters, maybe, but players who, on paper anyway, were more than capable of keeping the club in mid table and continuing to consolidate our position. These were, after all, players who had defeated one of the First Division's best teams.

I remember turning up for the final game of the season on 15 May. It was a bright, warm summer's day. Nature sometimes has no sense of occasion. In my screenplay, it would have been the dullest, wettest, most miserable and bleak day imaginable. Relegation was already confirmed. In the programme, Mel Sutton wrote, 'it is difficult for me to write these notes such is the disappointment of the past week ... The results of the past two weeks have been devastating, no win in the Reds' last 7 league games — The simple fact has been that with the small squad we had we just could not afford to have players unavailable and that happened at crucial times'.

Football is both a cruel and a painfully ironic sport. For, who should our opponents be for that final pointless game? Rotherham United — ROTHERHAM UNITED!

What better way can there be to twist the knife than be reminded of that day four long years ago when we had demolished Rotherham United 7 - 1 to secure promotion. Someone, somewhere, must have had a good laugh at that one. 1978's past glories seemed to be all around us, haunting us, that day. It was bad enough that it was Rotherham, but there, for the Yorkshire side, were former Liverpool captain Emlyn Hughes and also ex-Bristol City midfielder Gerry Gow. There were ghosts everywhere. I closed my eyes and I could see Graham Whittle slotting in his two penalties, Mike Thomas drilling a left-foot shot low into the net and somersaulting towards the Kop, Bobby Shinton carving out a goal from an impossible position, John Lyons side-footing in another, Graham Whittle's header, and Les Cartwright's majestic solo run and goal. Great memories. I could hear the roars of the crowd racing on to the pitch at the final whistle to embrace and salute their heroes. Wonderful memories. Sad memories as I looked at the empty acres of terracing on the Kop and paddocks and more red seats than people and the look of bewildered disinterest on the faces of those who had bothered to come to moan and/or mourn in the sunshine.

I think Wrexham won the game 3 - 2. The result was of no importance whatsoever. It was the strangest match that I had ever been to. It seemed somehow wrong to cheer when Wrexham scored.

Relegation meant that Mel Sutton's long service with the club was brought to an end as his contract was not renewed. Through the glorious 'Seventies, Mel's presence had been one of the constants through the cup, European and League successes. He was not a spectacular player, in fact, he was very under-rated; a hard grafter and a good ball-player who never let Wrexham down in the heat of battle. Another link with the double year was severed.

So, why spend time talking about relegation in a book celebrating the giant-killings? I suppose the bottom line is that it has to be this event that enabled Wrexham to still be classed as giant-killers. If we had maintained the great momentum of 1978 and swept through the Second Division, clearly we would have become one of the giants. Equally, if we had maintained our place in the Second Division, it would be stretching things a bit to keep on considering ourselves to be 'giant-killers'; second favourites for a cup-tie would have been more of an appropriate description when playing a side from the division above. To put it bluntly, Wrexham would not be British football's greatest modern giant-killers if the club had not spent most of the last 25 years outside of the top two divisions. The relegation facilitated this.

Arfon Griffiths wrote philosophically in the 'Promotion Special' programme in 1978, 'the downs last a long time and the ups seem very short'. And that's it really, isn't it? Peaks and troughs, highs and lows. Giant-killings are generally like brief shooting stars that appear from the darkness, shine briefly, then disappear back into the night which, after that burst of light, seems darker than before. The Forest game was an amazing triumph. The fact that it was achieved in such an awful season for the Reds, only serves to heighten the achievement.

NOTTINGHAM FOREST 1 v 3 WREXHAM
Venue: The City Ground
Attendance: 15,649

NOTTINGHAM FOREST:
Peter Shilton, Viv Anderson, Bryn Gunn, David Needham, Willie Young, Stuart Gray, Jurgen Roeber, Ian Wallace, Peter Ward, Mark Proctor, John Robertson
Manager: Brian Clough
Scorer: Proctor

WREXHAM:
Eddie Niedzwiecki, Phil Bater, Wayne Ciegelski, Steve Dowman, Joey Jones, Billy Ronson, Frank Carrodus, Steve Fox, Mick Vinter, Dixie McNeil, Ian Edwards
Manager: Mel Sutton
Scorers: Dowman, Vinter, McNeil

Referee: D. Richardson

WREXHAM v FC PORTO
EUROPEAN CUP WINNERS' CUP, 1ST ROUND, FIRST LEG
Tuesday, 19 September, 1984

While the issue of whether or not to be in Europe may overload the brain cells of virtually every politician in Britain, the issue has never been in doubt at any football club. And Wrexham FC is certainly no exception.

Those nights of European Cup Winners' Cup action at the Racecourse were very special and it is the club's involvement in this competition which gives the Reds' cup-fighting tradition an added dimension over almost every other small club. The closest that most 'minnows' can get to experiencing the heat of continental competition would be a night-in with a chicken tikka masala watching the *Eurovision Song Contest*.

Through the Welsh Cup, Wrexham were able to live the dream of all small

English clubs. And, of course, in 1976, Wrexham came so close to causing a sensation when they reached the quarter-finals of the Cup Winners' Cup, losing narrowly 2 - 1 on aggregate to the brilliant Anderlecht.

That really was the summit of Wrexham's overseas adventures. We could breathe the air of impossible European greatness. In the first round, Wrexham took on Sweden's finest, Djurgardens, and after a 2 - 1 victory at the Racecourse, went through following a 1 - 1 draw in Scandanavia. The Polish side, Stal Rzeszow, were the next to arrive in north Wales and left needing to overturn a 2 - 0 deficit. Again the Reds' proved their durability and resilience earning a 1 - 1 draw behind the 'Iron Curtain'. And so little Wrexham were propelled into the media goldfish-bowl of the quarter-final. For the first leg, Wrexham travelled to Anderlecht, a team of pure international class, and in front of 35,000 fans went down 1 - 0. It was a result that Liverpool would not have been too dissatisfied with. Wrexham were outstanding, not just equalling the quality of their Flemish foes, but out-playing them at times. In the return leg, nearly 20,000 fans packed into the Racecourse daring to dream of a semi-final place and, when Stuart Lee side-footed into the net to level the aggregate score, destiny seemed to be smiling. Wrexham dominated the game but, with 13 minutes left, a Dutch international by the name of Rob Rensenbrink broke many a Welsh heart. It was a great piece of skill: A run down the left, the cut inside, the low shot to the far post, Brian Lloyd's despairing dive, the rebound off the post, the ball in the net …

'It was only the sheer brilliance of Robbie Rensenbrink that beat us in the end', John Neal later recalled. 'That goal he scored was absolutely brilliant'. The crack Belgian team went on to crush West Ham in the final 4 - 2. 'They absolutely murdered West Ham in the Final', Neal added. 'They certainly did not murder us though. One of their officials said after the first leg in Brussels that whoever won the tie would win the Cup'.

Imagine what could, would have happened if Wrexham had beaten Anderlecht. It really is a beautiful thought. Looking back, it is almost surreal to think that Wrexham stood on the (Rensen) brink of the semi-final of the European Cup Winners' Cup. It is, I believe, still the only time that a British side from the Third Division has reached this stage of a major European competition.

It is also worth reflecting that Wrexham's performances in Europe over the years meant that they were often a SEEDED team. In 1990, Wrexham were seeded fourth, in front of Manchester United! UEFA later changed their seeding criteria to base it on the track record of any of the participating country's entrants over a five-year period. And with that change, the status of being a seed was lost. However, for me, the fun really went out of being in the Cup Winners' Cup with the introduction of the 'foreigners' rules. It was difficult enough to take on the likes of Man United or Romania's Petrolul Ploiesti (do not ask me to pronounce it) with a full strength squad, but to be forced to field, at best, half of the normal team … 'Stupid Rules', I thought at the time. But when I look at the 'United Nations' Premiership today, I fear for the future of Welsh international football and I do begin to think that the faceless UEFA rulemakers may have had their hearts in the right place after all.

Of course, the route into Europe itself was blocked off in 1995. They say that you never know how much you miss something until it's gone. Sometimes that's true. But, I certainly was not alone in savouring those special European nights at the Racecourse.

On 19 September 1984, Wrexham held the Welsh dragon high once more as they caused one of the biggest upsets in the history of European football when they beat one of the beautiful game's finest, FC Porto.

As the pedigree Portuguese giants arrived in north Wales for the first leg, there was every reason for them to believe that their place in the second round was a racing certainty. After all, they had reached the final of this cup the previous season, losing narrowly to the awesome Juventus. Their team had eight full internationals and included the 1983 Golden Boot sharp shooter Gomes. Porto was a club with seemingly infinite resources, regularly watched by crowds of 70,000. Wrexham's average home gate was now a meagre 1,600 hardy souls

The Porto president expressed his heart-felt hope that his stylish side would not beat the Welsh underdogs by too many goals. It was a nice thought. And it was, not surprisingly, a view endorsed by all but the most optimistic of home supporters as we made our way up to the Racecourse that night. Wrexham manager Bobby Roberts' assessment of the task facing his men could be seen in his team selection — six recognised defenders and a goalkeeper in his starting line up. There was a rumour circulating that, in training, the team had been shown a video of *The Alamo* to prepare themselves psychologically for the tie.

'We can give them a game', Wrexham captain Jake King announced on the day of the match. It was hardly a John Wayne-style rallying cry to motivate the masses. But, then again, Wrexham did not go into this game on a great wave of optimism. If the Anderlecht game represented the summit of Wrexham's achievements, for the Porto game, the club was somewhere below base camp.

These were desperate and dark days for the Reds who were languishing in the lower regions of the Fourth Division. The club was in crisis having plummeted from the dizzy heights of the Second and Third Divisions in successive seasons. And the downward slide showed few signs of slowing and, with significant debts hanging around the club's neck, the trap-door to non-league football or even financial collapse and extinction seemed all too real.

I remember attending the home game against Sheffield United on 26 February 1983. 'SOS, Save our Soccer', the programme cover read. 'This is an URGENT APPEAL to all persons/companies interested in Wrexham Football Club to attend a very important meeting … on the occasion of the launch of the unique Wrexham trust fund … to offset the interest charges paid by Wrexham FC … please, please be there!! … bring along however much cash/cheque you can loan …'

Many of us were convinced that there would soon be a minute's silence before a game to commemorate the passing of the light at the end of the tunnel. In 1983, I hit the magical age of 18. The child who had gone along to the Racecourse expecting nothing but victory had now evolved in to the man who expected nothing. I had become a pessimistic optimist. Or was it an optimistic pessimist? At any rate, this was my adult armour which is now, in 2001, very weathered and worn but which has served me well. In the promotion season, there was almost a danger that I was beginning to take the giant-killings for granted. Giant-killings should always be savoured for their unexpectedness.

Bobby Roberts had been appointed during the previous season and was trying to run the club on the threads of a shoe-string. As he settled into the dugout that night for his first taste of European action, his thoughts must surely have drifted back to a bitterly-cold night last November. Then it was that Roberts had quite literally played a major 'hand' in the Welsh Cup campaign which had provided this European platform. An injury crisis at the club had compelled the manager, at the age of 43, to play in goal against Alliance League part-timers Worcester City. And Roberts was certainly in the firing line as he made a number of crucial saves to enable his struggling side to cling on for a 1 - 1 draw. Thoughts of Europe were far from the minds of the fans who trailed away from the Racecourse as they were convinced that a victory in the replay was about as likely as Trevor Brooking joining Wrexham Supporters Club or of Boy George captaining Millwall. As it was, the Reds pulled off a major shock and defeated the non-leaguers and then proceeded to march on to the Welsh Cup Final, only to lose to Shrewsbury Town. Funny old game!

So the scene was set for a classic David v Goliath cup tie to be played on this international stage: two clubs who, in terms of ability, success, experience, wealth and geography were many, many miles apart … Game on.

From the outset, it was clear to the 4,935 fans ('What's it like to see a crowd?' the Kop sang to themselves) at the Racecourse that the players in red shirts were determined to live up to the club's proud European traditions — Wrexham had never lost a home European tie. Our team swarmed all over the pitch, giving the technically superior Portuguese no time to settle on the ball and play their neat passing game. But, in addition to the anticipated aggression and harrying, there was also unforeseen and, previously, rarely-demonstrated skill and creativity from the home side.

Incredibly, Wrexham could have been 2 - 0 up within the first 15 minutes. First, big Scottish target man Jim Steel rose high above the Porto defence to power an arcing header against the Tech End crossbar. Minutes later, the enthusiastic Kevin

Rogers burst through the defence onto a neat flick from striker David Gregory, only to fire disappointingly wide with only goalkeeper Borota to beat. The decibel level increased as we dared to hope that the impossible could just be possible. The game became an exhilarating flow of end to end attacking football, with the artistry and speed of the Cup Winners' Cup runners-up more than matched by the eleven red heroes who were playing their hearts out. The rookie Barry Horne, who was showing the potential which was to ultimately lead to the Welsh captaincy, was an inspiration in midfield. Jack Keay and Steve Wright were giving the performance of their careers in defence keeping the lethal Gomes in check. And upfront, the tactic of sending high balls into the Porto penalty area was allowing Steel, ably assisted by the innovative Gregory, to cause constant chaos.

As the first half drew to a close, there were narrow escapes at both ends. Steve Wright mis-directed a Porto corner against his own crossbar and, shortly afterwards, Gomes finally shook off his shadows to crack an unstoppable shot against the post.

Wrexham responded immediately and, when Horne broke clear, Borota hacked down the free signing from Rhyl outside the penalty area. The Yugoslav international, hands apologetically behind his back, explained to the referee that it might have been a bad tackle but it was the best one he could manage in the circumstances, and received a yellow card. But the Reds' opportunity was gone. The half-time whistle brought a huge, appreciative roar from the home crowd. Wrexham were winning — 0-0!

During the break, there seemed to be two questions being asked by supporters (the first one being common to fans of all giant-killing teams): Why can we not play like that all the time? And can we keep this up for another 45 minutes?

When Belgian referee Jean François Crucke got the second half underway, only the latter question would be answered as the Fourth Division strugglers continued to equal the enterprise of their high class opponents. Young defender, Shaun Cunnington, was proving to be a revelation in his new midfield role, breaking down Porto attacks and

Jim Steel putting the Porto defence under pressure. [Wrexham Leader]

launching fresh Wrexham raids. However, as the half progressed, the quality of Porto became more evident. As Wrexham began to slowly fade, so the blue and white stripes began to create more penetrating assaults on the home goal. Now, every Porto player looked like Pele. While the commitment of the Wrexham players remained resolute, you could almost see their self-belief beginning to fall away, legs that had been constantly chasing were becoming not so able and the crosses which had been so effective were no longer being delivered with the same accuracy.

The crowd became quieter. This was now a more familiar Wrexham we were watching. It seemed inevitable that Porto would score. But football is anything but predictable and on a surprise (to Wrexham) Wrexham counter attack, the tireless Horne honed in on a square ball from Keay and hammered a first-time 20-yard cracker against the underside of the bar. The ball ricocheted away but it seemed to be the turning point. The November gloom suddenly lifted, the floodlights seemed brighter, and Porto looked humanly frail once again. The Racecourse roar began once more and the red shirts rediscovered their confidence and energy.

With just 15 minutes remaining, Bobby Roberts sent on the young midfielder John Muldoon to try to inject some extra pace and width. Five minutes later, north Wales went into orbit. Steel controlled a long ball from defence on his chest just inside the Porto half and skilfully hooked the ball over his shoulder down the right wing and galloped away towards the box. Muldoon collected the pass and, as I watched from the Mold Road Paddock, he flew past us down the touchline towards the Kop. As he reached the by-line, Muldoon floated over an inch-perfect cross. The flying Steel rose unchallenged at the near post and directed his header past the stranded Borota into the net. What a goal! The Racecourse erupted. I do not think that so much noise has ever been made by 4,935 people. 1 - 0.

'The ball came in and I saw the goal line right in front of me', the £10,000 signing from Oldham later explained. 'It took a while for me to realise that I had scored but when it sank in, I could not stop dancing'. The final minutes, as in any great cup tie, saw many finger nails devoured as Porto desperately tried to salvage their credibility. 'Are you Chester in disguise?' sang the Kop, but the local subtleties of that song were probably lost on the visitors.

Goalkeeper Stuart Parker made excellent saves to deny both Gomes and Inacio as the Portuguese superstars piled on the pressure. But this was to be Wrexham's night and when the referee finally agreed with the whistling fans and ended the agony, incredible emotional celebrations began. The heartache of the two previous seasons and the current precarious position of the club were forgotten that night, by all except Bobby Roberts who reminded his ecstatic players that they had a difficult match on Saturday away at Crewe (Wrexham lost 3 - 0).

'We expected to win', Roberts was later to reflect quietly on his side's amazing victory. 'No one else did, just us. There was no pressure on us and the longer the game stayed at 0 - 0, the more I felt we looked as if we'd win it'.

'This is the best day of my life', said David Gregory. and then added quickly, 'except for my wedding day'. Other married supporters agreed that this was the best day of their lives. Every Wrexham player had been superb that night and thoroughly deserved their moment of glory. The outstanding move which created the goal simply underlined this magnificent performance and unbelievable result. But the job was only half-done. Porto coach Artur Jorge assured the amazed watching world that, 'we slightly under-estimated Wrexham, but we are the better team and we will prove that in Portugal'.

I believed him and began to work on my 'Europe's fine but we need to concentrate on the League' speech. Bobby Roberts quickly worked out that Plan A for the return game would be all out defence and try to nick an away goal. And, on a rainy night in the Estadio Das Antas on 3 October, Wrexham swiftly moved through to Plan D as the home side raced into a 3 - 0 lead before half-time. I sat in darkness at home listening to the Marcher Sound commentary. I was going to save myself the pain of the second half, but the Reds kept battling away and two goals from Jake King hauled the score back to a respectable 4 - 2 as the game entered its final dramatic minutes.

Then, John Muldoon picked up the ball on the right-wing and, with time running out, hit a long, hopeful cross towards the Porto goal. There seemed little danger but, from nowhere, Barry Horne hurled himself at the ball and volleyed an amazing, spectacular goal. The silence of the 30,000 crowd was deafening. There was no time for Porto to respond. They won the battle 4 - 3, but the aggregate score was 4 - 4, with the mighty Reds winning the war on the away goals rule.

Porto, one of the top five sides in Europe at that time, were knocked out by the Fourth Division men from north Wales. Under UEFA rules, clubs retained all of the gate receipts from their home games only. As such, Wrexham, a club already with major financial problems, made a loss of some £5,000 on the Porto tie. But what price glory?

The second round draw pitched Wrexham against the Italian giants, AS Roma, the previous season's European Cup finalists (beaten by Liverpool on penalties); a classy side stuffed full of Italian and Brazilian (Cerezo and Falcao) internationals. Porto were big, but Roma were huge.

As it was, 3 men were to prove to be the difference between the Serie A millionaires and the Fourth Division paupers: Laszlo Padar; A. F. Martinez — the referees; and Paulo Falcao. Roma won their home leg 2 - 0 and came away from the Racecourse with a 1 - 0 victory — Wrexham's proud unbeaten home record was ended. There was not three goals difference between the two sides. Wrexham were magnificent and deserved some better refereeing decisions than they got, a very dubious penalty and a clear offside being the two key goals in the first leg. Mr

Jake King heads one of the Reds' precious away goals against Porto.
[Wrexham Leader]

Falcao, though, the talented Brazilian midfielder who starred in the 1982 World Cup finals, was a class act. While all around him in the Roma Amateur Dramatic Society were being hassled and harried, he had all the time in the world; the sure sign of 24-carat class. Officialdom aside, it was Falcao's performance alone in the second leg that stood between the Reds and potentially more glory. As a lover of football, you had to allow yourself to enjoy watching him. It was a privilege to be in the company of greatness (one of my most treasured souvenirs is the Roma away programme signed by Falcao).

Another epic European adventure came to an end. The season ended with Wrexham in mid-table obscurity. In April 1985, the Reds parted company with Bobby Roberts.

In the games with Porto and Roma, it really had been like the old days again, cup fever in the town, national media coverage, international recognition for the club. With our idol from those days, Dixie McNeil, appointed as the new manager, this seemed to me symbolic that the good times were about to begin again. I certainly never imagined that, when the next giant killing actually came along, those good old days would be another seven years older.

WREXHAM 1 v 0 FC PORTO
Venue: The Racecourse
Attendance: 4,935

WREXHAM
Stuart Parker, Jake King, Shaun Cunnington, Neil Salathiel, Jack Keay, Steve Wright, Mike Williams (John Muldoon), Barry Horne, Jim Steel, David Gregory, Kevin Rogers
Manager: Bobby Robert
Scorer: Steel

FC PORTO
Petar Borota, Joao Pinto, Inacio, Eduardo Luis. Eurico, Quim, Frasco, Jaime Magalhaes (Ademar), Gomes, Paolo Futre (Micky Walsh), Vermelhinho
Manager: Artur Jorge

Referee: J. F. Crucke

WREXHAM v ARSENAL
FA CUP, 3RD ROUND
Saturday, 4 January, 1992

' … and then, unbelievably and catclysmically, we were knocked out of the FA Cup by Wrexham, who had the previous season finished bottom of the Fourth Division as Arsenal finished top of the first.' —Nick Hornby, *Fever Pitch*

There are days that you remember for a long, long time. And there are days that you can never forget.

Will anyone who was there ever forget that day when they saw the Robins' phoenix-like rise from the ashes of a ten season nightmare which had seen the club suffering relegations, virtual non-participation in the FA and League Cups, and battling not just for Football League survival, but for actual survival. And what a way to announce the club's return, with one of the greatest, if not the greatest of all, giant-killings in football history.

So what had gone so badly wrong for the club since those golden, heady days in 1978 when everyone believed that our Third Division champions would sweep through the Second and take their place with the elite in the First Division.

Of course, there is no one simple answer. Some conspiracy theorists point to Wrexham's decline beginning with Margaret Thatcher's election as Prime Minister in 1979! With hindsight, though, it seems clear that the team of '78 had reached their peak. But no-one can say that, under Fred Tomlinson's chairmanship and Arfon Griffiths' management, Wrexham lacked ambition. During the club's four year stay in the Second Division, major signings were made to bolster the squad and pursue the dream of becoming one of the giants in the top flight. Joey Jones (£210,000), Mick Vinter (£150,000), Ian Edwards (£125,000), Billy Ronson (£100,000), Ian Arkwright (£100,000), Steve Fox (£90,000), Frank Carrodus (£70,000), and Steve Dowman (£75,000) to name but a few. A new, impressive stand was also constructed at the Tech end to provide a better international venue. But the club was unable to ever really consolidate its position in the Second Division, let alone push on for promotion. A series of long-term injuries and fixture congestion due to a hard winter of postponements saw the first season become a struggle (six players needed operations and 24 match postponements). Bombarded with a horrendous backlog of fixtures, the momentum of the club buckled.

The injury jinx continued the following season with a number of careers (including giant killing stalwarts Graham Whittle and Mickey Evans) sadly ending prematurely. The departure of key play-makers Mike Thomas (to Manchester United) and Bobby Shinton (to Manchester City) meant that the club had two hard acts to follow. Many of the Reds' signings proved to be less than the envisaged spectacular success. And, as the team failed to make an impact, so the large crowds (unemployment was near to 20% in the area) and the much-needed revenue which they brought with them disappeared.

In reaching for the sky, the club fell. Weighed down by the debts which had been incurred in the Robins' Icarus-like flight, Wrexham plunged straight to the Fourth Division. There had been a few tiny glimmers of light during these times with the occasional European excursion and a play-off final under Dixie McNeil's management (unfortunately in the pre-Wembley days). But they had been false dawns.

When Brian Flynn took the helm in November 1989, the club still remained on the financial knife-edge and he had to see the Reds through a nail-biting relegation battle which eventually saw Colchester United taking the dreaded fall into non-league football.

The following season, restructuring of the League meant that there was to be no relegation from the Fourth Division. The Wrexham boss used this breathing space to give youth a chance and allowed his promising raw recruits to gain valuable first team experience. Wrexham ended the campaign bottom of the Football League and made a loss of some £72,000. But the value of that learning experience was to pay dividends in the years ahead.

An early indicator that the tide had begun to turn soon came as the Reds made it to the third round of the FA Cup. In the first round, non-league Winsford Town were swept aside 5 - 2, with young striker Steve Watkin grabbing a hatrick. It was Watkin who also supplied the only goal in the Reds' second round tie as they struggled past renowned non-league 'giant-killers' Telford United in front of a 3,897 crowd at the Racecourse.

The third round was very kind — a home tie against Arsenal, the League champions. The draw offered a vital financial boost for the club (Wrexham, to their credit, ignored any urge to switch the tie to Highbury) and an opportunity to gain revenge for the injustices suffered in that 1978 quarter-final. Except that for most people, well, those like me who were pessimistic optimists, thoughts of revenge and giant killing were hardly ignited. What was to make the victory over Arsenal so extra special was that it was so totally unexpected. Yes, Wrexham still clung on to their reputation as renowned cup fighters, but, in 1992, the games which had built that reputation were very distant memories. Nottingham Forest was incredibly ten long years ago.

'Arsenal might have a bad day and we would have to play above ourselves and perhaps then we could see a soccer miracle', said veteran midfielder Mikey Thomas, whose nomadic career had now brought him back to the club that had made him, on the eve of the momentous game. But, after those ten long, long dark years in the wilderness, there had been so much disappointment and despair and so little hope that, in truth, I doubt many Reds' fans honestly believed that the team had any kind of realistic chance. But revenge, like Wrexham Lager, is best served cold.

It was a cold January day. Over 13,000 people turned up at the Racecourse to watch the third round clash. Both sets of supporters were in good voice as the teams emerged from the tunnel. That magical moment, five minutes to three on third round Saturday, where so many raw emotions collide: hope, fear, doubt, excitement, anticipation, as the build-up and the waiting comes to an end.

Wrexham started brightly, passing the ball around the field with confidence. The yellow shirted Gunners remained in their own half of the pitch as the Reds produced their relaxed passing football with shot after shot reigning in on goal. But then the warm-up was over and it was time to kick off …

For the next 45 minutes, the First Division champions, attacking the Tech End, dominated the game with Merson, Campbell and Winterburn all being denied by some exceptional goalkeeping by the inspired Vince O'Keefe. In the opening minutes, the Reds' Wayne Phillips cleared Alan Smith's shot off the line and Jimmy Carter fortunately fired wide inside the penalty area with the goal at his mercy. And so the relentless pressure went on. O'Keefe and on-loan Manchester United defender Brian Carey were outstanding, they had to be.

'We were a bit fortunate not to be 3 - 0 down in the first 20 minutes', admitted

Another Wrexham raid on the League champions' goal.
[Wrexham Leader]

Wrexham's former Welsh international Gordon Davies after the game. The previous season had ended with these two teams 91 places apart in the Football League. Arsenal attacks were repelled by a combination of determined, desperate, fortunate, fearless defence. No-one could deny the sheer class of the Gunners which was epitomised by David Rocastle. The talented midfielder ran the show with his precision, punishing passing and tremendous vision. But Wrexham heads never dropped in the face of this superiority. In true cup-fighting tradition, the Reds kept on battling away, countering Arsenal's skill and speed with passion and pride. And the fans responded, cheering every tackle, every clearance, every touch of the ball. Wrexham even had a chance to score. Watkin fed the ball to left-winger Karl Connolly who then instinctively found Gareth Owen surging forward in space. Owen collected the ball and fired the ball narrowly past Seaman's left-hand post. The Kop collectively groaned but enthusiastically applauded their team's enterprise. But any hopes we had that the tide was beginning to turn in our favour were short-lived. On the stroke of half-time Merson beat Sertori, cut into the penalty area from the left-wing and fired in a low ball to the near post where England international striker Alan Smith was on hand to steer the ball from close-range past the helpless O'Keefe. 1 - 0 to Arsenal.

The half-time whistle came moments later. On the balance of play, no-one could deny that the League champions deserved their lead. Only 1 - 0 down. It could have been much worse. But so close to half-time, it had seemed that it was going to be so much better. Discussions for the break seemed to focus on whether this goal would be the start of the avalanche; could the Reds keep the scoreline to a respectable level; socio-economic reform in Russia; and the heat-retaining qualities of the local Bovril (OK, I lied about one of these).

As the second half progressed, a clear pattern of play began to emerge: Arsenal controlling the flow of the game with their slick, mean passing, Wrexham continuing to hustle and chase, never willingly surrendering territory but unable ever to jump into the driving seat and, in all honesty, not looking like they were going to create a decent scoring chance to light up the winter gloom. Arsenal seemed content with their neat play and single goal lead. A 1 - 0 defeat would not, of course, have been a disgrace for Wrexham.

But, if the League champions were sitting back and 'trying to play it as a training match' (as Gordon Davies later observed), they still nearly doubled their lead in the 62nd minute when full-back Nigel Winterburn fired in a cross-cum-shot which completely deceived O'Keefe and clattered against the underside of the Wrexham crossbar and away to safety. The relieved Kop roared their approval of this exquisite piece of luck. I doubted that they could have made anymore noise if Wrexham had, by some miracle, scrambled an equaliser. I equally doubted that I would get the opportunity to find out.

Looking back, there is no doubt that this was the turning point of the match. Fuelled by their good fortune, each Wrexham player visibly grew in confidence and self-belief. And at the same time, for some reason, each Arsenal player seemed to wilt. Soon after, Andy Thackeray broke through and hammered in a shot which Seaman palmed away. The ball flew to Davies who drove it disappointingly, to put it mildly, straight back to the grateful England international 'keeper.

Wrexham had fired their first warning shot. Our spirits were warmed. Arsenal were beginning to experience some real pressure and self-doubt for the first time in the game. The Arsenal supporters could see the game transforming and tried to rally their team. But their anxiety only spread to the players on the pitch.

'A lot of them were complaining all afternoon,' said Gordon Davies after the game. 'When you're big stars and things do not go your way, they tend to get a bit rattled.' Winterburn and Dixon picked up yellow cards for their collection as the Fourth Division side took the game to the giants. Arsenal players began to question virtually every blow of the referee's whistle. Always a good sign. We dared to dream of the impossible.

I am not sure if Einstein's theories of time addressed the issue of how quickly it passes when your team is losing, but the 20 minutes following Winterburn's near-miss flew by. Time was fast running out for impossible dreams. Then, in the 82nd minute, from a long clearance upfield, David O'Leary climbed on Gordon Davies' shoulders to head the ball away. The referee, that nice Mr Breen, knew a foul when he saw one and he saw one. Arsenal players and supporters naturally protested. George Graham later referred to it as a 'mystery' freekick (Wrexham had more than their fair share of mystery decisions to question in a certain FA Cup quarter-final in 1978 — we will call it quits). While his team-mates continued to bemoan the state of the planet generally and Mr Breen's eyesight specifically, David Seaman was focused on the job in hand — organising his wall. Some 20 yards away, towards the left hand corner of his penalty area, 37-year old Mikey Thomas, Wrexham's giant-killing veteran, was carefully placing the ball on the ground. If this had been *Question of Sport* and the action had been frozen at this point, I do not think that I would ever have guessed what was to happen next.

There was a sharp blow of the whistle. Thomas swooped like a preying eagle and unleashed the most perfect left-footed shot imaginable. The ball whistled past Seaman's despairing gloved hand up into the top right-hand corner of the net. There was almost a second's satellite delay of disbelief as the home supporters took in the enormity of the remarkable event they had just witnessed. It was in! We had scored! Wrexham had equalised! 1 - 1!

Or as a Channel 5 commentator might have eloquently summarised the event: GOOOOAAAALLLLLLLL!

The home crowd exploded into wild celebrations. I do not think that there is a single word that can adequately begin to describe that level of elation. But no-one realised, no-one could have imagined, that this was only the *hors d'oeuvres* and that the main giant-killing course was about to be served.

Arsenal were visibly shaken. Their composure simply evaporated in the fever-pitch atmosphere. What had been easy for them, now became impossible. They just could not keep possession of the ball. Wrexham were on a high and just grew stronger. Two minutes later, Owen found Davies down the right wing from Thackeray's throw. The experienced Davies took the ball in his stride and crossed dangerously towards the 6 yard box. Arsenal captain Tony Adams was first to the ball but stumbled as he attempted to clear the danger. The ball ran loose. Before Adams could recover, young striker Steve Watkin slid in first, his right foot cleverly hooked around the ball and directed it back at an acute angle towards goal. Seaman was completely wrong-footed and helpless as the ball rolled agonisingly past his despairing dive and rolled on towards the goal ... towards the goal. . just inside Seaman's right-hand post ... and. ... Goal! Yes! Goal! 2 - 1 ... 2 - 1 ... 2 - 1 ... 2 - 1!

Wrexham were in front. The crowd went berserk. The players went berserk; diving on top of N° 10 Watkin after his clinical opportunistic wonderful, wonderful strike. The earlier disbelieving excitement became, well, simply a crescendo of even more disbelieving excitement. It was all just so unreal.

But now, as well as rapture, there was an edge to the electrified atmosphere in the ground. And the edge was fear. All through the game there had been nothing to lose. At 1 - 1 or even 1 - 0 down we were still the brave, battling, undisgraced underdogs, the Fourth Division strugglers giving a good account of themselves against the multi-millionaires. Now there was a mind-blowing 2 - 1 victory against the League Champions to lose. No pessimistic armour could protect me now. Tangible hope had stripped away any pretence that I could stay detached from the outcome. I had to suffer like thousands of others as the Reds tried to protect a fragile, mortal one goal lead for those agonising, tortuous minutes.

Arsenal threw everything at Wrexham in those final ageing minutes and seconds of the game as the Reds clung on to their lead and their headline in history. The champions did indeed 'score' again but the linesman's flag had been raised long before Jimmy Carter put the ball in the Kop net. Welsh devastation and horror quickly turned to ecstatic, noisy, triumphant relief at the same time as north London ecstatic, noisy, triumphant relief turned to devastation and horror as everyone realised that the 'goal' had been disallowed. The Racecourse was an incredible emotional rollercoaster.

Then, suddenly, it was all over. Wrexham had won. The League Champions had been beaten. A fantastic explosion of noise swept up into the night sky. The joy, the elation, the pride. The footballing cliché is that we were 'over the moon'. Of course it's a cliché but you do know what people mean when they say it. In fact, it seems almost a betrayal to try to describe the emotions which swept through our bodies in those minutes immediately after the final whistle. To define them seems to bound them in limits. The fans rushed onto the turf to celebrate and carried their red-shirted heroes shoulder high off the pitch. 'Brian Flynn's red and white army', they sang over and over again. Life does not get much better than moments like this, uncomplicated, perfect, gravity-defying joy. This was the greatest giant-killing of all time.

It would be a mistake to say that in those glorious celebrations, the many disappointments and frustrations of the previous ten years were forgotten. They were not. They could not be. They should not be. The tears in the eyes of many of the people there confirmed to me that they were an integral part of this moment. They were the canvass on which this masterpiece was created. Without them, the magic could not have been so special, so spell-binding. The depths of that decade were the measure of the heights of this triumph. George Graham surveyed his lowest point in management philosophically. 'It's a big blow', he said. 'I've been in the game long enough to realise it's about highs and lows. We've had a few high periods and now we're having some low ones'.

In those heady minutes following the game, I found some time to think of those devastated human beings at the Tech End. I knew their despair, all football supporters know it. We have all been on that long miserable journey home. Those Arsenal fans would never have contemplated defeat, why should they? I felt it only right to give them a few moments of my thoughts — I had, after all, expected that from them in 1978. I also expected them not to begrudge too much our moment of glory.

Trauma for them was just a trophy-less season. It certainly was not about the battle for Football League existence. I knew that their depression would not last too long. And, of course, it did not. In 1993, this side won both the FA Cup and League Cup. In 1994, they collected the European Cup Winners' Cup. And surely the fact that these Arsenal players went on to such achievements only confirms again how special this 1992 giant-killing really was — and still is.

That night, I drove my wife to despair. I guess I must have punched up Teletext, how many times I cannot say, but we did have to buy new batteries for the remote control the next day! Page 301 — the sports headline. Page 303 — the wonderful story. I read the words and read them again. Sheer poetry. Old Bill Shakespeare never managed to write them like that. But this was not just a sports story. This was *the* news story! Every news had to be watched, and recorded of course. Everywhere was that big headline with the word 'WREXHAM' there for everyone to see and hear speaking to the whole of Britain, telling the whole world that THE giant-killers WERE BACK.

Wrexham, my team, had defeated the mighty League Champions. If I had been a cat I would have dislocated my purring muscle. And then came *Match of the Day*. 'What a great theme tune', I enthused as the video rolled. And there was Mickey Thomas firing that precision thunder-bolt and Steve Watkin's lightning instincts and we had won it all over again, and again, and again, and again, and again, and again, and again and, you have to marvel at technology, don't you?

And then came Sunday. With the mother of all hangovers to contend with, there was the complete range of Sunday newspapers to savour and leisurely consume like fine red wines. Thomas 82, Watkin 84 — they were excellent vintages. Every word, every picture was there to be enjoyed. And when the stories were read and every page explored for any further references to this momentous event, the reports would be lovingly re-read once more … I must have been hours in that newsagents.

And the next day at work, I found myself on a crusade; a dual- purpose mission to remind everyone that I am, was, and ever will be a Wrexham fan and, of course, to seek out as many Arsenal fans as I could. Finally, thoughts turned to the draw for the fourth round. All that Wrexham could ask for was a home draw, the club had not won away from home in the League since October 1990.

So, as you would expect, they were drawn away, at another 'giant', West Ham

United. It was to be the end of the Wembley road. But not until two more fantastic performances had been added to the club's cup-fighting CV. Wayne Phillips and Lee Jones produced quality finishes to earn a deserved 2 - 2 draw at Upton Park. The replay saw 17,995 turn up at the Racecourse. A first half header from the Hammers' Colin Foster was enough to separate the First and Fourth Division sides. There were some 'interesting' refereeing decisions which did not help the cause. But let's concentrate on the positive.

Wrexham were back. The cup run provided much-needed cash for the club and self-belief for the young players. The talents of young striker Lee Jones were also showcased in the second round and Liverpool were persuaded to part with £300,000 to secure his services. The finances for the club were changing slowly for the better.

Manager Brian Flynn and Mark Sertori celebrate the cup win against Arsenal with a 'cup of tea'. [Wrexham Leader]

And what a difference a season makes, the Fourth Division became the Third Division as the Premier League was born. And on the 27 April 1993, Wrexham won 2 - 0 away at Northampton Town. The scorer of both goals was fittingly one Gary Bennett; the outcome of that game was the three points necessary to clinch promotion to the Second Division. For the final game of the season, there was a red and white carnival. The Colchester United players formed a guard of honour to applaud the Wrexham players into the sunlight. The Kop was packed and everyone was smiling and singing, 'E-I, E-I, E-I-O, Up the Football League we go', over and over again. At the end of a thrilling 4 - 3 Wrexham win, the players did a three-sided lap of honour to celebrate their runners-up position before the crowd poured onto the pitch to party.

You just do not forget days like those. You cannot.

WREXHAM 2 v 1 ARSENAL
Venue: The Racecourse
Attendance: 13,343

WREXHAM:
Vince O'Keefe, Andy Thackeray, Phil Hardy, Brian Carey, Mike Thomas, Mark Sertori, Gordon Davies, Gareth Owen, Karl Connolly, Steve Watkin, Wayne Phillips
Manager: Brian Flynn
Scorers: Thomas, Watkin

ARSENAL:
David Seaman, Lee Dixon, Nigel Winterburn, David Hillier, David O'Leary, Tony Adams, David Rocastle, Kevin Campbell, Alan Smith, Paul Merson, Jimmy Carter (Perry Groves)
Manager: George Graham
Scorer: Smith

Referee: K. Bree

WREXHAM v IPSWICH TOVVN
FA CUP, 3RD ROUND
Saturday, 7 January, 1995

'It was a classic,' enthused Reds' manager Brian Flynn after this thrilling third round giant killing. 'In many ways it surpassed the Arsenal game. This tie had the lot with goalmouth incidents, good football and a penalty winner. I haven't seen a game like it in a long time. We played well and when they came back at us we defended by the skin of our teeth.'

Brian Flynn was in his sixth year as manager and had experienced as many footballing highs and lows as any Wimbledon match ball. Ipswich manager, and former player, George Burley, was only eleven days into his new job at the Suffolk club who were struggling at the foot of the Premiership and he, too, was finding out that life was anything but boring. Ipswich's last three games had seen them defeated 2 - 0 by Arsenal and 4 - 1 by Everton, but their launchpad for the Cup had been a resounding 4 - 1 win at home to Leicester City. In these games, Burley had used 16 players as he shuffled his pack in search of a winning combination and many Reds' fans were wondering if the Premiership side were now turning the corner.

On the eve of the game, Burley was emphasising the importance of victory for his team, with a good cup run boosting players' and supporters' morale in their relegation fight. However, Wrexham's firmly-established cup tradition and the Portman Road club's apparent vulnerability had led many to anticipate a 'shock' at the Racecourse and some pundits had even made Wrexham, currently lying in 13th position in the Second Division, the favourites. Brian Flynn, though, was quick to put things in perspective. 'Our visitors might not be having the best of times in the Premiership, but the quality of their individual players must not be under estimated'.

While, in comparison to the Premier League big guns, Ipswich were a club of modest means, they had assembled an experienced, talented and not inexpensive squad which was laced with international players: Bulgarian international Bontcho Guentchev, Uruguayan international Adrian Paz — a £1 million signing, £750,000 buy Ian Marshal, Steve Sedgeley (a £1 million buy from Spurs), Welsh international Geraint Williams — £650,000 from Derby and big centre half David Linighan, a £300,000 signing from Shrewsbury. Linighan, in particular, should have known all about Wrexham's giant-killing abilities — his brother Andy could have told him all about the day he played in north Wales in January 1992 for Arsenal.

Wrexham's most expensive squad member was goalkeeper Andy Marriott, a £200,000 signing from Nottingham Forest. Otherwise, the Reds consisted of home-grown talent and free or nominal value transfers. When I think of Ipswich, I think of Arnold Muhren and Co. hitting the heights in the top-flight. In Ipswich I always saw Wrexham, a small town club of limited financial clout, and I knew that my dreams were indeed possible.

In their Second Division campaign, Wrexham had failed to achieve the level of performance and consistency that players, fans and management knew they were capable of, having taken only 34 points from 22 games. Ultimately, the team would finish disappointingly just outside the play-off zone.

In the FA Cup, however, Wrexham had put in two excellent performances to reach the third round melting pot. The first round had brought the efficient and effective Stockport County to the Racecourse and, in a tough game, only Steve Watkin's goal separated two very well-matched teams. The second round draw gave the Robins a home game against another fellow Second Division side, Rotherham United, and Karl Connolly turned on the style as he inspired the Reds to overturn the Millers' early goal and achieve a 5 - 2 victory, scoring two goals himself with Bryan Hughes, Gary Bennett and Steve Watkin also finding the net.

The Cup draw again favoured Wrexham with a home draw and, even better, gave them a tie with a 'giant'. It was the first time that Wrexham had ever met the blue shirts of Ipswich town. And the pleasure was to be all Wrexham's.

In the opening minutes of the game, though, doubts were quickly sown into the minds of any supporters expecting an easy 'kill'. Ipswich left no-one in any doubt that they were not intimidated by the Robins' reputation as they took the game to the home side and attacked with pace and aggression. The lively Kiwomya, the Suffolk club's top scorer for three of the past four seasons, looked dangerous at every opportunity as his pacey runs pulled Humes and Hunter out of the centre of the defence. Kiwomya briefly silenced the home crowd when he chased a long ball forward and, almost opened the scoring, when his clever looping back-header had the advancing Marriott scrambling backwards to just claw the ball up onto the crossbar. The Kop breathed a collective sigh of relief as the danger ended with the ball being launched to the safety of Row Z of the Yale Stand.

This close-shave seemed to spark the Reds into action. Gareth Owen began to assert his authority in midfield and Karl Connolly on the left wing began to weave his magic. Cross and Durkan also began to make surging runs towards the Ipswich goal, with the goal hungry Gary Bennett prowling the penalty area. For the next half-an-hour, Wrexham produced some controlled, attacking football as they sought to breach the Premier side's supposedly frail defence. The hard-running Cross worked tirelessly alongside Bennett but Linighan and the 37 year-old Scottish international veteran John Wark provided stubborn, impenetrable resistance, with reserve goalkeeper Baker also in commanding form. The Reds' best chance of the half fell to Bennett when Connolly slipped the ball invitingly across the penalty area only for Wrexham's one man goal-machine to stall on this occasion as his shot flew wide.

At half-time, with the score at 0-0 and our team in control, the 8,000 home fans gave the players a loud ovation. With Wrexham kicking into the Kop end in the Second half, the return of the two teams was eagerly awaited … we knew there would be goals

As the game restarted, the Reds were in no mood to allow their opponents to get back into the game as they surged forward to intensify the pressure on the Premiership goal. Gareth Owen was an inspiration in midfield covering every inch of grass, challenging for every loose ball, winning every battle. But he was not alone as the whole team worked for each other to create that vital, decisive opening. Bennett, the bargain free-signing from Chester City, and Cross were both frustrated by the impressive Baker.

But Wrexham were not to be denied their golden moment. In the 59th minute, Cross coolly took control of the ball on the left, just inside the penalty area, and headed for the by-line. As defenders careered towards him, the young striker waited and then chipped over the perfect cross to the far post where 19 year-old Kieron Durkan honed in to crash a fantastic, unstoppable right foot volley into the back of the net past the diving Baker. 1 - 0!

Durkan raised his hands in celebration to the Kop as his team-mates surrounded him. 'Wem-ber-ley, Wem-ber-ley' sang the ever-hopeful faithful as the red shirts maintained their tight grip on the game in pursuit of the killer second goal. There was a vibrant atmosphere in the floodlit ground as the Reds attacked and attacked but final passes went agonisingly astray as the blue shirts' crowded defence held on.

With fifteen minutes of the game remaining, it started to become apparent that the brave Reds were beginning to tire. The tide turned as Ipswich began to threaten the Wrexham goal as they saw the chance to get that precious equaliser. Tony Humes, who had spent 9 seasons with the Suffolk club before joining Wrexham, and Northern Ireland international Barry Hunter had to be at their battling best in the heart of the home defence to maintain the 1 - 0 lead.

Anxiety in the crowd was rapidly and visibly spreading onto the pitch. Every time the ball was cleared up the field, Ipswich were quickly able to regain possession and launch another attack.

It is always a good idea to remember that there are more important things in life than football. In the tense, closing minutes of a third round FA Cup tie, it is hard to recall what they are. With finger-nail supplies all but exhausted, disaster struck. There were only five minutes left when Ipswich swung over a corner from their left-wing and Linighan, who had been their best player all afternoon, rose unchallenged by the penalty spot to direct a powerful header down to Marriott's right and up into the net. 1 - 1.

It was a sickening blow. And, if I'm honest, I probably expected the blue shirts to steal a winner. Pessimism rules OK! But, incredibly and miraculously, disappointment quickly turned to elation again for Wrexham. Almost straight from the kick-off, Wrexham won a seemingly innocuous free-kick in midfield. Ipswich regrouped in determined defence. Owen fired the ball forward towards the right corner of the penalty area where the effervescent Connolly was waiting. The talented winger controlled the ball calmly on his chest and in one slick Bergkamp-like movement knocked the ball past Adam Tanner. The young defender panicked and hacked the flying Connolly to the ground.

'PENALTY! 'screamed the crowd — The referee agreed. The Ipswich players did not protest.

The crowd had gone from despair to ecstasy in just over a minute — and from ecstasy to nervous hope as their goal-hungry hero Gary Bennett stepped up to carefully place the ball on the penalty spot. 'I tried to think of it as just another penalty,' said Bennett later. 'But I realised as I stepped up that this was probably the most important penalty I shall ever take'.

Bennett tore in and drove the ball low to Baker's right. The keeper guessed correctly and got his hand to the ball. I was standing on the tips of my toes on the Kop looking down to my right. I did not see the ball, but I saw the net ripple. Baker did not need to look up. The Racecourse roar confirmed to him — and me — all that we needed to know. 2 - 1.

Bennett raced towards the Kop, ripped off his shirt and thrust it into the air in

Gary Bennett.

front of the delirious, worshipping fans on the terraces. It was a memorable moment. I have seen many better goals at the Racecourse but never a better, more heart-felt goal celebration. It was Bennett's 28th goal of the season and his 90th goal for the club in less than three seasons.

But the 'fun' was still not over. Before the Kop could begin another joyous chorus of 'Wemb-er-ley', Ipswich swept forward again from the kick-off. What seemed like hours of desperate defending followed as the Premiership side threw menacing crosses into the penalty area. Then, in the distant goal-mouth scramble, the ball ricocheted out of a group of players towards the Wrexham goal. Miraculously, Marriott managed to get his fingertips to the ball to deflect it up onto the underside of the crossbar and away to safety. I watched, scarcely able to breathe, as the frantic drama unfolded at the other end of the pitch. No matter how many games you watch, each time, you still feel so helpless; so powerless. But it's only a game of football, I tried to tell myself.

The relief at the final whistle was unbelievable. Yes we had rode our luck on a couple of occasions. But there should be no doubt that this was a thoroughly deserved victory — another hugely entertaining cup-tie, another proud display, another famous giant-killing.

Sure, it is only a game of football. But what a feeling when you hear that final whistle and your heart and soul embrace the achievement. Sure, it does not change your life, but it certainly paints it a nicer colour for a while.

Wrexham's reward for this win was an away tie at Manchester United. Eric Cantona may have been serving his suspension for his Bruce Lee impressions down at Selhurst Park, but United were still the top Premiership team. While there was to be no fairy tale at the Old Trafford 'Theatre of Dreams', the golden-shirted Reds put on another entertaining display. The final score was 5 - 2 to the Premiership champions but that did not tell the story.

Kieron Durkan coolly fired Wrexham into the lead in the opening minutes in front of a disbelieving Stretford End. United hit back with devastating effect before Jonathon Cross grabbed a spectacular goal in the final minutes, memorably beating Schmeichel from 20 yards.

The defeat marked the end of Wrexham's cup romance for another year. But this was an occasion never to be forgotten. The thousands of Wrexham fans were determined to enjoy their day — Old Trafford is without doubt the next best thing to Wembley. And the team certainly gave them a performance to sing about. It would have been all too easy and excusable to have tried to close the game down and defend. However, Wrexham really went for it, surging forward at every opportunity.

Wrexham's performances against these two Premiership opponents had enhanced their reputation and earned them many new admirers. United manager Alex Ferguson was quick to praise the Second Division side's performance and acknowledged that his all-star international side had been more than a little embarrassed at times by the quality of Wrexham's football.

WREXHAM 2 v 1 IPSWICH TOWN
Venue: The Racecourse
Attendance 8,324

WREXHAM:
Andy Marriott, Barry Jones, Phil Hardy, Bryan Hughes, Tony Humes, Barry Hunter, Gary Bennett, Gareth Owen, Karl Connolly, Jonathon Cross, Kieron Durkan
Manager: Brian Flynn
Scorers: Durkan, Bennett (pen)

IPSWICH TOWN:
Clive Baker, Adam Tanner, John Wark, David Linighan, Paul Mason, Frank Yallop, Steve Palmer, Chris Kiwomya, Steve Sedgeley, Claus Thomsen, Bontcho Guentchev
Manager: George Burley
Scorer: Linighan

Referee: J. Rushton

WEST HAM UNITED v WREXHAM '
FA CUP, 3RD ROUND REPLAY
Saturday, 25 January, 1997

Remember that old fictional footballing cliché of the substitute coming off the bench in the dying minutes of a cup-tie to score the winning goal? For Roy of the Rovers, better read 'Russell of the Reds'!

League and cup clashes between Wrexham and the Hammers have, without exception, provided a feast of incident-packed attacking football and the FA Cup in particular has witnessed three monumental battles during the past two decades.

In 1981, the Robins, as members of the 'old' Second Division, entered the competition at the third round and were drawn away at the FA Cup-holders — fellow Second Division side West Ham. Wrexham trailed for most of the game to a controversial penalty and the cause looked lost until a spectacular volley from Captain Gareth Davis on the edge of the penalty box produced an 86th minute equaliser.

The first replay ended goalless. Manager Arfon Griffiths then won the toss to host the second replay at the Racecourse and in a truly epic encounter, deadly Dixie McNeil — who was actually playing at left-back because of injuries — pounced in extra-time to slot a left-foot drive past Phil Parkes into the Kop net and send the cup-holders crashing out 1 - 0.

West Ham, however, were to taste sweet revenge some 11 years later. Third Division Wrexham were on cloud nine (and probably ten and eleven as well) after their giant-killing of the mighty Arsenal and a cracking Wayne Phillips' volley and a late Lee Jones equaliser at Upton Park earned the Robins a fantastic 2 - 2 draw at Upton Park. In the fourth round replay, though, there was to be no further fairytale as the Premier team edged through 1 - 0.

As the two sides lined up in 1997, cup honours were therefore very much even. The Hammers were still a Premier League team, while Brian Flynn's men had remained in the Second Division. Wrexham were lying in 10th place in the Second Division, just two points outside the play-off zone, having taken 38 points (ten wins, eight draws) with home gates averaging around 4,000.

The Hammers were finding life to be very tough in the Premiership as they hovered just above the relegation zone. The FA Cup represented their only chance of success. They were certainly a side capable of going all the way. Manager Harry Redknapp had made some serious big money investments. And his impressive squad had the cosmopolitan feel of a United Nations peace-keeping force These included unsettled Romanian international Florin Raducioiu — a £2.4 million signing from Spanish side Espanol; Romanian international Ilie Dumitrescu — £1.5 million from Spurs; Croatian international defender Slavan Bilic — £1.65 million from Germany's Karlsrhüer SC; Richard Hall — £1.5 million from Southampton; Australian Stan Lazaridis — £300,000 from West Adelaide; Northern Ireland internationals Michael Hughes (£500,000 from Strasbourg) and Keith Rowland (£110,000 from Bournemouth); John Moncur — £850,000 from Swindon; and striker Steve Jones — £150,000 from Bournemouth. The Hammers' 'keeper was Czech international Ludek Miklosko. There was also Welsh international Mark Bowen and future England international defender Rio Ferdinand.

Wrexham had struggled past non-league Colwyn Bay in the first round. A Bryan Hughes' header thirteen minutes from the end made the score 1 - 1 and saved Wrexham's blushes. The replay (both ties played at the Racecourse) saw Hughes bag two more goals as Wrexham won 2 - 0. Third Division Scunthorpe United arrived in north Wales for the second round and twice took the lead in the 2 - 2 draw. In the replay at Glanford Park, Scunthorpe again took the lead twice, with Steve Morris grabbing the vital second equaliser in the dying seconds of the match when United goalkeeper had the kind of nightmare moment that even Freddie Kruger cannot conjure up when he completely sliced his clearance back towards his goal, leaving the alert young striker a simple tap-in. In the extra-time that followed, the dependable Steve Watkin tucked away a penalty to secure a 3 - 2 win and that third round home tie with West Ham.

Brian Hughes, Wrexham's goal scorer in the drawn tie against West Ham at the snow-bound Racecourse.
[Wrexham Leader]

History between the Robins and the Hammers suggested that a replay would be necessary to settle this encounter. History was right.

On a snow covered pitch in front of nearly 10,000 spectators, the Reds took the lead as early as the sixth minute when Bryan Hughes was the quickest to react to Carey's knockdown and direct a diving header inside the post past the stunned Miklosko. The claret and blues were stung into life by this goal and, inspired by the dynamic Julian Dicks, fought back strongly. When Marriott, under intense pressure — or a foul as the rule books neatly define it — from striker Steve Jones, was unable to collect a high ball on the edge of his penalty area, Porfirio was on hand to place an inch-perfect chip into the top right-hand corner of the net.

At half-time, the score was 1 - 1. In the second period, both teams put on an excellent display in the difficult conditions, with both 'keepers being called into action to keep their sides in the cup. There were no further goals and most agreed that a draw was a fair result. After the game, however, the gloss was taken off the Reds' impressive display as Hammers' boss Harry Redknapp slammed the 'scandalous' state of the snowbound pitch and criticised the referee for allowing the game to go ahead. 'It's ridiculous playing on a pitch like that ... It was like something out of the 1970s.' It was reported that Mr Redknapp then added, 'now Upton Park — we'll finish the job.' Famous last words.

That night, football expert and former Hammer Trevor Brooking was more than happy to confirm to *Match of the Day* viewers that a decent London pitch would enable the Hammers to win through. After all, he reasoned 'this is an important cup tie, especially for West Ham'. No bias there then.

The replay was set for Wednesday, 15 January, but heavy fog in east London caused the game's postponement. Both Messrs. Redknapp and Brooking had no doubt forecast bright sunshine such was their obvious talent for predictions. The replay finally went ahead on Saturday, 25 January, in near-perfect conditions for the time of year and Harry's — and Trevor's — bubbles were about to be blown away.

Brian Flynn's men — in the club's lucky white away shirts — started in confident mood and Owen quickly tested Miklosko with a firm drive. The Hammers, who were struggling to collect points in the Premiership, were in no mood to roll-over and allow the underdogs to take control.

The ever-dangerous Steve Jones went close on two occasions and, from a corner, there was mayhem in the Robins' penalty area until a well-aimed boot provided welcome relief. West Ham looked dangerous from every set-piece with Williamson's flighted corners into the danger zone and Dicks' well-rehearsed free kicks causing more than a little anxiety amongst the away fans.

But the Wrexham defence did not yield. Captain Humes was in fine combative form and Carey stood tall to repel the Londoners' advances. Full-backs McGregor and Hardy remained solid in defence and were also quick to support numerous counter-attacks. In midfield, Gareth Owen and Bryan Hughes were not giving an inch. At half-time, the teams remained level at 0-0 and Wrexham went off to thunderous applause from their travelling fans. The home side had created the better chances but Wrexham had not been out-played and there was everything still to play for.

The second half began as an even tussle with both sides looking creative in attack and resolute in defence. Chalk should have done better, after Connolly cleverly found him, than fire at the Hammers' Czech goalkeeper. Marriott then did well to cling onto a powerful Bilic header and the lively Bishop blazed over the bar after some fine Portuguese trickery from substitute Porfirio. Neither side seemed able to find the clinical finish which would propel them into a fourth round tie against the waiting Peterborough

As the minutes flew by, Wrexham began to take the game more to their Premiership opponents and, from an Owen corner, Carey's header fell to Chalk. His shot was blocked but the ball broke loose to Hughes in the six-yard box. With the goal at his mercy, the free-scoring midfielder unbelievably fired wide. There were roars of disappointment from the Welsh fans behind the goal as the best chance of the match was missed. But the Second Division side's heads did not drop and they continued to match the Londoners for skill and determination. Reds' coach Joey Jones was to observe, 'if a neutral had walked into the ground, they would have had great difficulty telling which side was from the Premier League'. Joey, of course, is not one of life's neutrals.

With fifteen minutes of the game left, and the prospect of extra-time and even penalties becoming more of a reality, the hardworking Owen was replaced by substitute Kevin Russell. For the next fourteen minutes and forty seconds, Russell's contribution was steady but uneventful. But, as the final minute began to tick away, his contribution was about to become spectacular.

As the ball rolled out of play midway inside the West Ham half, the impressive McGregor collected the ball and, with his throw-in, found Chalk in space. Chalk needed no further encouragement to cut inside towards the retreating defenders. At the right moment, he fed the ball in to the cool Watkin on the edge of the area. The blonde striker looked around for support from the attacking white shirts and then, almost casually, rolled the ball into the path of the rampaging Russell. Without hesitation, the right-footed substitute looked up, 20 yards out, took aim and struck the sweetest left-footed dive. The ball flew low to Miklosko's right. And then, there was the ball nestling in the Hammers' net — a beautiful sight. 1 - 0!

The fans behind the goal went crazy. The bald-headed Russell, in his second spell with the club, continued his run to the advertising boards, with the rest of his team in hot pursuit, to celebrate with the dancing fans. Ex-Hammer and England World Cup hero Geoff Hurst looked on from the stands. Even he must have known that, this time, it really was all over. There was only time for a few brief, tortuous moments of West Ham pressure and then the final whistle came — another famous victory. The serial giant-killers had struck yet again.

After the game, Russell of the Reds — and his left foot — was the centre of attention. 'He normally uses that for standing on', joked Andy Marriott. It was,

Steve Watkin negotiates the snow and the West Ham defence. [Wrexham Leader]

however, left to Trevor Brooking to put the game, the result, and the Reds' fine performance in (his) perspective on *Match of the Day* — West Ham had lost the match because of behind-the-scenes troubles in the boardroom. Thanks, Trevor!

The rockin' Robins were now flying, and a thrilling 4 - 2 victory at Peterborough United (United twice taking the lead) quickly followed with Russell adding another two superb strikes to his collection.

The fifth round tie at First Division Birmingham City saw the white-shirted Reds undeservedly fall a goal behind in the first half to a Steve Bruce volley. But after the break, Wrexham became again that great giant-killing machine as Hughes, Humes and Connolly struck to send the club into the quarter-finals again.

The Sunday papers had a field day as they began to wonder if the Wembley show-piece was destined to be an all-Second Division clash between Wrexham and the conquerors of Nottingham Forest, Chesterfield.

But the draw was to quickly remove that mouth-watering prospect. Wrexham's was the last name to be drawn. Another away tie. But surely it had to be third time lucky for us as Wrexham were drawn against their fellow Second Division side — a club which had never before reached the dizzy heights of the last eight of the world's greatest cup competition. Added spice was given to the tie when it emerged that Chesterfield, whose star striker Kevin Davies would be suspended for the game, were trying to sign the 'uncuptied' striker Gary Bennett from Preston. But the up-front Bennett was to place himself even further in the heart of every Wrexham supporter when he stated, 'I'll guarantee one thing: There's no way I would play for Chesterfield against Wrexham in the FA Cup quarter-final. That is a non-starter as far as I am concerned. But the other way around, playing for Wrexham in the FA Cup quarter-final, is a totally different ball game'. Bennett's 105 goals in 150-odd appearances for Wrexham had already made him a living legend. This display of red-blooded loyalty enhanced his god-like status. And what do you know? Bennett and the fans got their wish. Brian Flynn's efforts to complete the signing of another ex-Wrexham striker, Lee Jones from Liverpool, fell through. And the deadly striker we called 'Psycho' was back in town.

While the game was to be played at Saltergate, the whole of north Wales was swept up on a tidal wave of cup fever as a semi-final appearance beckoned. The re-signing of Bennett added to the explosion of excitement and expectation.

BBC Wales wished to televise the game live and, to accommodate this, the Sunday kick-off was rescheduled to 11.30*am*. At this point, I have to confess that a feeling of dread descended on me. I mean, I have to admit to normally looking forward to games with Chesterfield with the same level of enthusiasm as I have for answering the front door to sales reps or those who wish to pray for my soul in the living room. But it was more than this. As sure as Wrexham always start a season slowly, so they never seem to play well before 3*pm*. I could only think of past years at Stockport and Chester where the Reds had struggled to locate even first gear. I could only think of one occasion when Wrexham had even scored on a Sunday — and that event was hardly likely to engender a warm, rosy glow in my heart; the defeat at Orient in the Fourth Division play-off final. So, as the game drew closer and talk of Wrexham's 'Wembley Way' grew louder, I tried to tell myself that there had to be a first time.

But for a third time there was to be a cup full of quarter-final misery for us. Like 1974 and 1978, this was to prove to be a 'Crying Game' as Wrexham lost by just one goal again; this time losing 1 - 0. A fatal hesitation in the second half between Deryn Brace and Andy Marriott enabled Chris Beaumont to loop the ball agonisingly into the empty net. But, while that was the match winning — or losing — moment, the fact is that the team just did not play. Wrexham had come from behind on many occasions during this campaign but you just knew that it was not going to happen on that Sunday. The team simply did not do themselves justice and, crucially, in the second half Chesterfield did, and therefore deserved their glory. Brian Flynn summed it up in a few words when he said, 'It hurts — but it has been a memorable cup run'. I hate quarter-finals!

Chesterfield marched on proudly on to an Old Trafford semi-final where they gave an inspired 2 - 2 performance against Middlesborough before falling in the replay. For Wrexham, the psychological devastation of the result was not clearly visible. But it could be felt. Talk of making the play-offs disappeared as the remainder of the season drained away. And thoughts turned to next August and a new season of promise and perhaps another great cup run.

There will be another quarter-final, I know it. I just hope it's going to be fourth time lucky for us and then who knows?

WESTHAM UNITED 0 v 1 WREXHAM
Venue: UPTON PARK
Attendance: 16,763
WEST HAM:
Ludek Miklosko, Tim Breacker, Slaven Bilic, Rio Ferdinand, Julian Dicks, Frank Lampard,
Danny Williamson, Ian Bishop, Stan Lazaridis (Hugo Porfirio), Steve Jones, Michael Hughes.
Manager: Harry Redknapp

WREXHAM:
Andy Marriott, Mark McGregor, Phil Hardy, Tony Humes, Brian Carey, Martyn Chalk, Gareth
Owen (Kevin Russell), Bryan Hughes, Peter Ward, Karl Connolly, Steve Watkin.
Manager: Brian Flynn
Scorer: Russell

Referee: Steve Lodge

WREXHAM v MIDDLESBROUGH
F. A. CUP, 3RD ROUND
Saturday, 11 December, 1999

And there we were. Five minutes to five on an FA Cup third round Saturday evening. The seven-year old boy, the thirty-something father and the grandfather. Three generations united in football. Our hands ached with clapping. Our throats raw and sore with shouting and cheering. But, most of all, our hearts full to overflowing with joy and pride.

Before the match, all the talk across the media had been about the changing face of football and how the FA Cup had lost much of its importance and magic. There we were on the brink of the 21st Century, a whole new millenium, so talk of new beginnings was, of course, blowing in the cold winter wind. But there we were at the Racecourse ground and the jubilant scenes all around me and the pounding beat of joy within me were satisfyingly familiar. Now, do not get me wrong, I have no problem with change in itself. Change can be good. We were sitting in the newly-opened million pound Pryce Griffiths Stand that now graced the long-neglected Mold Road side of the ground — a welcome new development.

The scheduling of the third round had been brought forward to accommodate the enlarged European programme in the New Year — some moaned, but I liked the revised date.

And change can be bad. Manchester United, the holders of the Cup had opted out of defending their trophy this season in favour of a FIFA package tour to South America and a world club tournament sideshow. The words I had read and heard from the great and the good were about the FA Cup being devalued, fatally wounded and how the traditions of this great event were a thing of the past.

Well, undoubtedly they were right. In principle, a competition which does not feature one of its top sides and players is not the challenge or the spectacle that it could be. But I had not been involved in an objective debate. I had just lived through the thunder and lightning storm of an FA Cup tie between a small Second Division club and a £35 million Premier League squad of international superstars. The sum extent of the FA Cup existed for me only in that tiny corner of north-east Wales. And I had not been alone. From the draw through to kick off, cup fever had again been virilent with 11,000 tickets being devoured by Reds' supporters. The Cup was about Wrexham and Middlesbrough. Those were the teams that mattered. This was the magic — as vibrant and fresh as it had ever been.

Some 25 years ago, Middlesbrough had been there at the beginning, one of Wrexham's first scalps. They had returned now as even higher-flyers and their defeat again in one of the most exciting football matches I had ever seen proved one thing above all others, that the currency of the world's greatest club competition had not been devalued.

Apart from the occasion and the result, there had been one more aspect of the Cup that had been so very familiar. And that was Wrexham's seemingly inevitable struggle to conquer lower division opposition. The first round had brought non-league Kettering to Welsh soil and striker Neil Roberts' goal was the only bright spot in a highly fortunate 1 - 1 draw. For the replay, BSkyB sniffed a 'giant killing' and televised the tie live but early goals from Steven Roberts and Danny Williams secured a 2 - 0 victory.

The second round brought Third Division Rochdale to the Racecourse and strike duo Neil Roberts and Craig Faulconbridge produced the goals in an unconvincing 2 - 1 win and a place in the lucrative third round draw. And the draw was kind. Very kind indeed. The men from the mighty Riverside Stadium were coming.

Looking ahead to the game, manager Brian Flynn commented, 'It's another big occasion and another big test. But we have proved in the past we are capable of raising our game against big clubs … The FA Cup is a wonderful competition. It rouses players and fans alike. These are games to be enjoyed'.

With my now usual lack of confidence, I was fairly sure that this was more likely to be a game to be endured. Yes, we had beaten Arsenal and Ipswich and West Ham in the '90s but the Middlesbrough set-up looked pretty daunting. Former Man United and England captain marvel, Bryan Robson, was the manager of Boro. Last season, they had finished a very creditable ninth in the Premier League and were looking a comfortable mid-table outfit again. The FA Cup represented their main avenue to the heady delights of European qualification. And Robson undoubtedly had the team to deliver cup success. In goal was 6' 5" Australian international Mark Schwarzer, a £1.5 million signing. In defence, prominent personnel included Italian Gianluca Festa, a £2.7 million signing from Inter Milan, and former Man United favourite and England international Gary Palister (£2.3m); midfield could boast England internationals Paul 'Gazza' Gascoigne and Paul Ince, German international Christiian Ziege (£4m), and Brazilian superstar Juninho whom Boro had sold in 1997 for £12 million , only for the prodigal genius to return on loan earlier this year. In the forward line, Boro had two giant strikers who resembled the famous Wembley twin towers themselves, Colombian international Hamilton Ricard and former Leeds United goalscorer Brian Deane.

On paper and on the television screen and on the pitch warming up before the game, the Premier League team looked formidable. They had even limbered up for this tie by dumping Arsenal out of the League Cup. 'The most important thing in any game is the manner you approach it,' said Flynn. 'You have to look at strengths and weaknesses and on the evidence I saw they have got very few flaws. But individuals have weaknesses … I remember the Arsenal game …' So did I. 1992 is a wonderful memory but I did not think my team had a hope of anything more than, at best, a glorious draw and a cash bonanza replay.

What else could any right-thinking pessimist foresee? After all, Wrexham were in the middle of a dismal relegation-threatening run and had not even won a game in the Second Division since August. We did not even have the weapon of surprise in our armoury. Boro boss Robson knew the job that lay ahead of his side. 'Wrexham have proved over the years that if you under-estimate them you may well get beaten. A few top clubs have lost there and we will give them respect,' he observed before steely emphasising that he expected his players 'to do a good enough job to see us through'.

As Boro lined up in a rocking Racecourse, only the injured Ince was missing from their batch of international superstars. Here it was. Three o'clock. The roar rose up to a rousing crescendo, the third round was here. Now. Throw your dreams and fears in the air and hope … the drama had begun.

The first half was a pulsating cup tie. Wrexham immediately raced through their gears and won a corner with their first thrust forward. The Kop roared their defiant belief in their team, a powerful, stirring act of faith. Wrexham responded with passion and skill. Faulconbridge and Neil Roberts were everywhere up-front while little Robin Gibson on the right wing caused a number of anxious flurries in the visitors' penalty area.

Middlesbrough, though, had too much quality and strength to be pinned back for long and soon began to settle down. Gascoigne and the mercurial Junino found space in the midfield and began to carve out chances for both of their white-shirted strikers. Reds' keeper Kevin Dearden made excellent saves to keep out Deane's header and Ricard's chip and then dived at the feet of the flying little Brazilian. Juninho really was the star of the show. Total class. Skill, vision, speed, he had everything and I found myself holding my breath everytime he got hold of the ball on any part of the pitch.

But Wrexham were not also-rans, Carey and 19 year-old Steven Roberts remained solid at the heart of the Reds' defence and, in midfield, Darren Ferguson was battling away and launching promising Welsh raids. Wrexham were very much giving as good as they were getting and both Russell and Ferguson had good chances to beat Schwarzer. But the opportunities were not taken and there was a collective sigh of relief when, soon after, full-back Phil Hardy was in the right place to clear Deane's back-post header off the line. As half-time approached, it seemed amazing that the game was still goalless. Wrexham certainly deserved to be on equal terms with their Premier opponents.

But that was not to be. The menacing Ricard appeared to first push into a Reds' defender and then handle the ball as Boro played a hopeful long ball up into Wrexham's box. The crowd howled for a freekick. Worse was to come as the ball broke loose to Deane whose shot at goal was deflected past the wrong footed Dearden into the net. Disaster. 1 - 0.

All eyes turned to the referee who was making his way back to the half-way line as white shirts celebrated. We could not believe it. He was allowing the goal to stand. 'Cheat' began to boom out from three packed sides of the ground. We were gutted, incensed at this cruel injustice. We felt cheated. As the whistle for the end of the first period followed some three minutes later, angry protests intensified. But, of course, the goal stood.

If anything, the noise that erupted at the beginning of the second half was even louder. It certainly had a greater intensity, an edge. This was now a battle not just to win a football match, but to right a wrong. It somehow felt a moral standpoint about fighting for the rights of all small clubs, to prove a point that we deserved to exist, to be on the same pitch as this wealthy team from another footballing planet. They had money in abundance, resources that we could never compete with. And now they had received the seemingly kind helping hand of the referee as well. Everything and everyone was against us. It was time to fight back. This was personal.

As the players emerged, I rallied to the cause along with 11,000 other voices. 'Come on you Reds'. We can do this. We must do this. There was no hiding place. An irrelevant competition? I do not think so. This was an explosive powder-keg and five minutes into the second half, our brave, fantastic reds gave us the spark we so badly desired.

Ferguson collected the ball on the left of midfield, looked up and delivered an immaculate pass into the path of the flying Gibson. Without breaking his stride, the little winger collected the ball and slammed in a low left-foot shot that beat the flailing, helpless dive of Schwarzer. It was a sensational goal! So sudden and so unexpected and so deserved. 1 - 1! Justice!

Gibson, Wrexham's instant hero, later recalled, 'I can't describe how I felt when the ball hit the back of the net. The noise that went up was unbelievable. It frightened me to death'. The game had been a tremendous all-action spectacle up to this point and now it went into over-drive. Boro were stung into life and rampaged up the pitch immediately to win a corner. In the ensuing scramble, Gascoigne found Ricard in space only for Dearden to deny him with another wonder save. But this was not the signal for a one-way procession of pressure from the Premier men. World stars many of them undoubtedly were, but they were matched by the passion, fight and skill of the team in red and white.

And then, a priceless moment. The talented Ferguson, whose confidence and influence on the game were visibly growing by the minute, took a quick free-kick midway inside the Boro half. He rolled the ball short to Kevin Russell and immediately received the ball back again. Ferguson was now on the move towards the edge of the opposition penalty area. As a row of defenders approached, he moved in-field and seemed to dance effortlessly past three or four white shirts with the ball magnetised to his trusty left foot. The goal was there 18 yards away straight in front of him and as Festa and friends moved in, Darren Ferguson pulled the trigger. The ball skimmed over the lush green turf and we all knew its destination before it arrived. The huge frame of Schwarzer again flew low to his right but there was no way that he or any other mortal goalkeeper could keep out such a sensational drive. The ball ripped into the bottom corner of the net. 2 - 1!

Wild, ecstatic celebrations exploded around the ground and probably across the whole of north Wales. Ferguson peeled away and ran across to salute the Yale Stand where his father, the manager of Manchester United, was watching. 'My dad doesn't see me score too many,' commented Ferguson, a free signing, on his first goal for the club, 'but he would have been pleased with that one. I took the ball inside and when it left my foot I fancied it to go in. I hit it perfectly'.

I have experienced some fantastic occasions at the Racecourse. But I do not think anything as special as the pounding atmosphere that now engulfed us. 'WREXHAM! WREXHAM!' Again and again. Every kick was cheered. Every clearance celebrated. All 11,000 people in complete bombastic union. Wonderful!

Wonderful and scary. For here we were again with our dreams in our hands and a long bumpy road still to negotiate. The inconceivable giant-killing was now so real. And what could we do? We could not kick the ball, or tackle, or anything. All we could do was shout and cheer and encourage those eleven men to give their all. We sang with all our hearts. They played with their hearts on their sleeves. Everyone gave everything to the cause.

We knew that there would be a backlash and it came. Juninho was the instigator of all Boro's best moves and he tormented our fragile nerves. There was some desperate defending but Boro found Dearden in outstanding form. His breath-taking reflex saves kept out efforts by Deane and Ricard. Dared we believe?

Then the silky Juninho played in the on-rushing Ziege through the centre of Wrexham's for-once out of position defence. The impressive German was clear through with only Dearden to beat. He had to score. We braced ourselves for the inevitable, the tragic. Ziege swept onto the ball with the ruthless efficiency of a German international and then, miraculously, blasted his shot high over the crossbar into the gratefully receiving Kop. There was a huge roar. No sarcasm, just plain, honest relief. Ziege knew that he had just wasted a 24-carat chance of redemption for his team and held his head in his hands.

For us, it was a sign. A sure sign that this was going to be our day. The chanting and singing and cheering began again with renewed vigour and, if not an undercurrent of confidence, then a definite feeling of positive hope. But that's not to say that there were no more heart-stopping moments. Of course there were. But that's an integral part of the magic. If the impossible was easy it would be prosecuted under the Trade Descriptions Act.

With the last throw of the dice, Boro won two late corners. This was it. The imposing presence of Schwarzer came forward and took up residence in Wrexham's penalty area. But we survived, survived with style. At the final whistle, hundreds of fans rushed on to the pitch in a tidal wave of celebration. Another truly memorable giant killing. The supporters had been such an important part of this victory that it seemed only right that they were there on the turf shoulder to shoulder with the players who had performed so wonderfully well.

So there we were in the Pryce Griffiths Stand, on our feet, applauding, singing, cheering, watching these fantastic scenes, savouring those special moments. On

Darren Ferguson and Robin Gibson, the goal scorers against Middlesbrough.
[Wrexham Leader]

Match of the Day that evening and in the papers the next day, there was no feeling of a worthless competition. Giant-killers dominated the back pages.

And of course the press had their story, the story of Ferguson & Son; the father whose team were not even taking part; the son who had been a match-winner. 'A memorable day, again,' said a thrilled Brian Flynn. 'Absolutely fantastic from start to finish. It was an enthralling cup tie and I thought we deserved to win'.

A slightly contrary view emerged from the disappointed Boro boss. 'I don't think they deserved to win because we had good chances and we let Wrexham back into the game'. But he acknowledged 'they showed good spirit and the crowd helped them'.

Reds' coach Joey Jones, who had played in the Wrexham side that had beaten Boro back in 1974, was also quick to acknowledge the part played by the supporters. 'Our fans were magnificent. Look what a difference they made. They lifted the lads. Their support gave our players that extra inch, that extra yard which is so important'.

The next round draw granted Wrexham another home tie. This time the opposition were Cambridge United, next to bottom in the Second Division. The ideal opportunity to progress to the fifth round, we might have thought. Wrexham lost 2 - 1. From complete euphoria to total disappointment. That is essentially the story for all giant-killers. But at least we have some fantastic memories. And there is always another season.

WREXHAM 2 v 1 MIDDLESBROUGH
Venue: The Racecourse
Attendance: 11,755

WREXHAM:
Kevin Dearden, Mark McGregor, Steven Roberts (Dave Ridler), Brian Carey, Phil Hardy, Robin Gibson (Gareth Owen), Danny Williams, Darren Ferguson, Kevin Russell, Neil Roberts, Craig Faulconbridge (Karl Connolly)
Manager: Brian Flynn
Scorers: Gibson, Ferguson

MIDDLESBROUGH:
Mark Schwarzer, Steve Vickers, Gianluca Festa, Gary Pallister (Jason Gavin) Robbie Mustoe, Paul Gascoigne, Brian Deane, Phil Stamp, Christian Ziege, Hamilton Ricard, Juninho
Manager: Bryan Robson
Scorer: Deane

Referee: Steve Lodge

FINAL THOUGHTS

There's a perfect blue May sky above and I am sitting there; all around me are thousands and thousands of people — an incredible mass of vibrant, cheering red and white. From the manicured lush green turf, my eyes look across, upwards at the awesome white twin towers sparkling in the sunshine. There seems to be no breeze but the Welsh Dragon is flying proudly, triumphantly as the soul-enriching *Men of Harlech* pounds into my head and my heart. And then, suddenly, the teams are emerging from the tunnel and there is too much noise to even hear the noise and too much raw emotion to even try to be anything other a part of this tidal wave of unprotected optimism and ...

I am no expert, but I think I know what that recurring dream is all about. Its about getting past quarter-finals. Its about being there. Achieving the ultimate prize. And we will.

There is a *Trivial Pursuit* question yet to be written which will read something like — 'Name the only two non-English clubs to have won the FA Cup'. Cardiff — is one of them. And that is ancient history. We all know who the other team is, don't we — WREXHAM IS THE NAME!

A GIANT-KILLING DREAM TEAM

Every supporter will have a different view as to who should be in a Wrexham dream team. Actually, I cheated and allowed myself to select a dream squad. There have been so many great players over the past 25 years (I cannot find room for Billy Ashcroft or John Roberts or Eddie Niedzwiecki or Andy Marriott or Brian Carey or Jim Steel or Dave Smallman or Mel Sutton or Chris Armstrong or Mark McGregor or Bryan Hughes or Joe Cooke or John Lyons or Les Cartwright or Steve Watkin … or Barry Hunter ….

Anyway, this is my side. You may disagree with me — fair enough. But all I know is this side would take some stopping. More than that, this team would play with breath-taking skill and passion, a team that would entertain and show why they call football 'this beautiful game', attacking at every opportunity with pace and flair, scoring goals that would make a Brazillian drool and a Mexican wave.

This team would not be giant-killers for very long because it would quickly take its rightful place in the land of the giants:

1. **DAI DAVIES** — a commanding figure who marshalled his defence effectively and loudly. Assured, experienced Welsh international (52 caps), dominating in the penalty area and a solid shot-stopper.

2. **JOEY JONES** — another experienced Welsh international and as whole-hearted and committed a defender as the club has ever had. The sort of character that every team needs with his tremendous humour and 'never say die' attitude.

3. **ALAN DWYER** — tough left-back with the pace and skill of a winger. No-one skinned Dwyer.

4. **GARETH DAVIS** — a brilliant reader of the game. An ever-present during the 1976–77 and 1977–78 seasons. Calm and reliable. A Welsh international who should have been awarded far more caps.

5. **EDDIE MAY** —the defensive wall! A reassuring figure at the heart of the Reds' defence. Commanding in the air, rock solid on the ground. A natural-born leader.

6. **MICKEY THOMAS** — yet another Wrexham-produced Welsh international (51 caps). A tenacious competitor, non-stop runner, creative and skilful, with the sweetest of left feet.

7. **BOBBY SHINTON** — the showman with the silky skills and the devastating finishes who could unlock any defence and embarrass any 'keeper. His 56 goals in 175 games for the Reds barely begins to tell the story.

8. **ARFON GRIFFITHS** — the midfield general; creative, dynamic and inspirational — a real class performer who deserved more international recognition. 17 full caps for Wales — Wales in the early '70s would have been far better off and more successful if Arfon had been on the pitch more often in the engine-room in the dragon red shirt. Wrexham's second highest all-time goalscorer —120 goals from midfield.

9. **DIXIE McNEIL** — the only striker who could keep Gary Bennett out of the starting line-up. On the ground or in the air, deadly Dixie was always there, the perfect predator. But Dixie's contribution to the team was always much more than his 88 goals in 222 games.

10. **GRAHAM WHITTLE** — two power-packed feet could turn a game with his spectacular goals from almost any distance. In midfield or up-front, Graham Whittle was a top class performer, whose shooting changed the course of matches. No-one in the history of football has ever hit a more emphatic penalty than the one he scored in the Blyth Spartans replay. 117 goals in 394 games and how many more would he have scored if injury had not forced him out of the game prematurely?

11. **KARL CONNOLLY** — a lethal left foot and tremendous in the air; a classic tormentor of defenders either on the wing or through the centre. 100 plus goals for the Reds cements his place in my team.

Substitutes

12. **BRIAN LLOYD** — excellent shot-stopper — a fine all-round 'keeper and a Welsh international.

14. **GARY BENNETT** — a goal-scoring legend at Wrexham, a fantastic finisher. The Reds have had so many excellent strikers over the years, but 'Benno's record speaks for itself — 100 plus goals in 170 games.

15. **BARRY HORNE** — a Wales captain. Endless energy, a hard tackler and an eye for goal.

16. **DARREN FERGUSON** — The Red Dragons' talented playmaker has been a consistent and inspirational performer. A strong character with a superb left foot whose match-winner against Middlesbrough is one of the great giant-killing moments.

17. **KEVIN RUSSELL** — up-front or in mid-field 'Rooster' has been an excellent servant for the club who has never let us down in the heat of battle.

18 **STEVE FOX** — there has never been a faster player at the club. Foxie could destroy any defence with his pace and skill and had the ability, but not the consistency, to be an England international.